Back to Basics: Insurance

by Jack Hungelmann

WILEY

Publisher's Acknowledgments

Senior Acquisitions Editor:
Tracy Boggier

Project Manager:
Chad R. Sievers

Compilation Editor:
Georgette Beatty

Technical Editor: Rhonda Graves

Production Editor: G. Vasanth Koilraj

Cover Images: (car) © ElenaLux /
Getty Images, (heart) © damlakaracetin /
Getty Images, (document)
© FrankRamspott / Getty Images

Cover Design: Wiley

Back to Basics: Insurance

Contents

1

Seven Guiding Principles of Insurance

I'm writing this book to help you take responsibility for your life. I'm writing for people who don't want to be victims — people who want the tools and information to be empowered when they make decisions. If that sounds like you, you're in the right place.

This book regularly refers to seven guiding principles, all of which are covered in greater detail in this chapter. Follow these seven principles when making decisions about your insurance program, and your decisions will be good ones.

Keep It Simple

Managing *risk* (the chance of a loss happening) and buying insurance is tough enough without making it any more complicated than it has to be. For every risk this book shows you, generally more than one strategy exists that effectively minimizes that risk. Using the principle of keeping it simple, you take the simple path. *Simple* means easier and more likely to be implemented — simple is not less effective.

Here's an example of how this principle can be used: Following a major fire or burglary, one of the requirements in a homeowner's policy is to create an inventory of what was lost or destroyed, including, if possible, any receipts and canceled checks. Does that sound like a nightmare to you? It is. Even harder than *documenting* what you had is *remembering* what you had. Imagine coming home from a hard day at the office and finding either charred remains of what was once your dream home or your front door broken and your home torn apart by a burglar. The emotional trauma is bad enough. But, in addition, you have to remember what's missing because you get paid for only what you can remember.

_____

_____

_____

A *policy* is the legal contract between you and an insurance company in which the company agrees to pay covered claims when you have them in exchange for a monthly (or some other periodic) payment from you. Any given policy contains many coverages.

Conventional insurance wisdom has always held that the solution to this dilemma is to fill out a household inventory booklet prior to any loss, listing descriptions and values for every piece of personal property you own in every room of the house. Talk about a fun way to spend an evening — or, more realistically, your two-week vacation.

A written inventory isn't such a bad idea, but it violates the principle of keeping it simple because it's complex, and it takes far too much time. As a result, it's rarely accomplished.

 A far simpler strategy for handling this documentation is a video or photographic inventory. This approach is easy and fast (you can film the whole house in an hour or two).

I particularly like the video strategy because everything you own can be recorded on one device, it's easily stored, and, best of all, you can easily add to it when you acquire new things. An extra benefit of having filmed documentation at claim time is a reduced need for receipts: Most adjusters will waive that requirement if they can see the item in your home prior to the loss, in some kind of photographic format. All in all, the video strategy is superior in every way to the written inventory strategy. Of course, if the house burns down, so will all your records, so be sure to store the photos or video safely off-premises (for example, in a safe-deposit box at your bank).

Don't Risk More than You Can Afford to Lose

I'm all for taking risks if it makes economic sense. Carrying large *deductibles* (the amount of a loss that you pay out of your own pocket before insurance kicks in) to lower insurance costs is a smart gamble if you save enough on your *premiums* (the price you pay for the insurance policy covering a defined time period — for example, six months or a year). Not buying collision insurance on older cars that you could afford to replace is another smart gamble. But be sure to insure any risk that is a part of your life if the risk could cause you major financial loss — if it's more than you can afford to lose.

For example, the financial hardship of your paycheck stopping as a result of a long-term illness or injury is substantial. About one-third of all workers, at some point in their career, have a long-term disability. Yet many people who totally depend on their paycheck don't have disability insurance. Big mistake — it's a clear violation of the principle to risk only what you can afford to lose. Disability insurance is the most under-purchased major insurance coverage in the United States. (*Coverage* is a promise to pay a certain type of claim if it occurs; other examples include automobile liability coverage, theft coverage, and so on.) If the loss of your income would cause major financial problems in your household, and your employer doesn't provide disability insurance for you, make sure you carry a good disability policy. (Chapter 8 explains what makes a good disability policy.)

Don't Risk a Lot for a Little

Spending a little now (for coverage) makes more sense than spending a lot of your own money later when something happens that you're not covered for.

_____

_____

_____

Most people who buy insurance can't afford to buy unlimited quantities; you probably don't have millions of dollars of liability coverage, for example. So you tend to buy a limit that feels comfortable and doesn't blow your budget. But too many people are considerably under-insured, and, tragically, they're seldom aware that better insurance would cost them very little.

Liability is your financial obligation to another person (or persons) for injuries or property damage you cause. Liability coverage is a promise in an insurance policy to defend you in court and pay what you owe another person (or persons) for injuries or property damage you cause, up to the liability limits you chose.

Using car insurance as an example, the most commonly purchased liability insurance limit in the United States today is $100,000 per person for injuries you cause to others. Is that enough to pay for a seriously injured person's medical bills and lost wages, as well as compensation for that person's pain and suffering? Just the medical bills alone could easily use up the entire coverage limit, leaving you to personally pay all other costs, plus some of your own defense costs. Your personal, uninsured financial loss could easily reach several hundred thousand dollars. Table 1-1 shows some typical annual costs for additional liability coverage for two cars in a metropolitan area.

Liability Limit	Additional Annual Costs beyond the Cost for $100,000	The Amount of Additional Coverage beyond $100,000
$300,000	$50	$200,000
$500,000	$80	$400,000
$1.5 million	$150	$1.4 million
$2.5 million	$225	$2.4 million

Table 1-1: *Typical Annual Liability Costs for Two Cars*

Following the rule to not risk a lot for a little means that you shouldn't buy only $100,000 of coverage when each additional $100,000 of coverage costs so little. In fact, you can usually pay for the extra cost simply by boosting your policy deductibles to the next level. Increasing your deductible by $250 to $500 often saves you enough on your insurance bill to pay for most or all of the added cost of additional liability coverage.

Consider the Odds

This rule says that when the odds of a claim happening are virtually zero, and the insurance costs are inappropriately high, you shouldn't buy the insurance. Considering the odds also means buying insurance when the possibility exists that a serious claim could occur.

Homeowner's policies exclude earthquake losses. But they do offer an option to buy the coverage for an additional charge. Here are two examples of how the principle of considering the odds applies: It's estimated that only about 20 percent of California homeowners had earthquake coverage to protect themselves against the devastating California earthquake of 1989, despite the high odds of an earthquake occurring. The 80 percent who were uninsured were in clear violation of both this rule (to consider the odds) and the rule not to risk more than you can afford to lose. As a result, many homeowners suffered ruinous, uninsured earthquake losses that easily could have been avoided with the purchase of insurance.

But if you live in an area that has no prior history of earthquakes and is located nowhere near any known fault lines, the probability of an earthquake may be near zero. In this instance, considering the odds means maybe not buying earthquake insurance if it costs more than a few dollars a year.

Like earthquake damage, flood and surface-water losses are excluded under the traditional homeowner's policy. Considering the odds means that if your home is located high on the pinnacle of a hill overlooking a valley and your basement is unfinished, you probably don't need to spend your money on flood insurance. On the other hand, if your home is located in a low-lying flood plain or near a river, you probably should consider buying flood insurance because the odds of a large loss are good.

Risk a Little for a Lot

This principle encourages you to avoid insurance when the risk is small in relation to the amount of the premium. Say, for example, you own a 1996 Honda worth $1,000. You were just hit with a DUI, and you're facing premiums of two to three times what you had been paying — not just this year, but for each of the next three to five years. Your collision insurance premium with a $500 deductible has just increased from $100 to $300 a year. If you keep this coverage, the maximum risk to the insurance company is the value of the car ($1,000) minus your deductible ($500) minus the salvage value of the car ($50), which totals $450. This rule advises you not to buy what turns out to be $450 of insurance for a $300 annual premium. Under these circumstances, the smart move is to drop the collision coverage.

_____

_____

_____

Avoid Las Vegas Insurance

Avoid any insurance that transfers only part of the risk to the insurance company, leaving you unprotected for the rest. Accidental-death insurance purchased from an airport vending machine is a good example; it often pays only if you die in a plane crash in the next few days. What you really may need is more life insurance, protecting you all the time and from any cause.

With Las Vegas insurance, you are, in effect, betting that if the claim occurs, it will be the result of a limited cause of loss you bet on. Table 1-2 shows some examples of Las Vegas insurance and a better alternative that gets rid of the gamble.

Type of Insurance	The Pitfalls	Better Solution
Accidental death	Pays only if you die accidentally	Life insurance
Travel accident	Pays medical bills only if incurred on a trip	Major medical health insurance
Cancer or dread disease coverage	Pays only medical bills caused by a specific calamity	Major medical health insurance

Table 1-2: *Types of Insurance and the Associated Risks*

The bottom line? If you buy any insurance that transfers only part of the risk — as these examples of Las Vegas coverage do — you leave yourself vulnerable. Spend a little more money, and get much better insurance.

Buy Insurance Only as a Last Resort

This principle advises you to buy insurance only when it's the best and most cost-effective solution. You have many options in treating any given risk; insurance is only one. Treat your risks with non-insurance strategies first. (See Chapter 2 for information on how to do that.)

Here's one example of how this principle works: Say you've inherited Grandma's heirloom sterling silver. It's precious to you, so, naturally, you want the best coverage possible. Your agent has you get an appraisal that costs you $100. You buy a special rider to your homeowner's policy covering the silver's appraised value of $10,000 at a premium of $90 a year. One year later, burglars break into your home and steal your precious heirloom. In the meantime, the silver has increased in value to $15,000. You collect the $10,000 insurance proceeds from the policy, but you've suffered three disappointments:

- The $5,000 difference between the value of the stolen silver and the amount that insurance covered.

- Grandma's pattern has been discontinued and it's difficult to find an identical match.

- Even if you find the same pattern, it doesn't have the sentimental value that Grandma's *exact* set had.

Insurance is not the best solution for managing this risk — not only because cash is a poor substitute for treasures, but also because of the hassle and cost of the appraisal, as well as the insurance premium that's due every year.

A better, non-insurance, method for handling Grandma's silver risk (and at the same time following the strategy of keeping it simple) is to store the silver in an off-premises safe-deposit box, thus preventing the loss almost entirely. Or, if that isn't practical because you want to use the silver for special occasions, hide it well, reducing by about 90 percent the chance of a loss through theft. You can further reduce the risk by adding a central burglar alarm.

When it comes to irreplaceable treasures, preventing the loss altogether is a far better strategy than insurance, without the costs or the pitfalls of insurance coverage.

_____

_____

_____

2

Managing Your Risk without Buying Insurance

The goal of this book is to provide you with the tools you need to effectively manage the personal risks in your life. Insurance is an effective way of managing risk, but it's not the only way. You can identify risks and treat them with creative, non-insurance strategies — and you should do so whenever possible, instead of limiting yourself to buying insurance. Non-insurance strategies reduce your insurance costs and are often more effective than their insurance counterparts.

Many people throw insurance at every problem. They inherit a stamp collection worth $50,000, and they buy more insurance. They rent a car on vacation and buy insurance for that car. This chapter fills you in on a different and better way of doing things: risk management. The essence of risk management is to treat risks with non-insurance methods first and to buy insurance second. This chapter starts by giving you four non-insurance strategies for reducing risk. Then those strategies are put into action with a real-life case study.

The ARRT of Risk Management

When it comes to risk management, there are four non-insurance strategies you can put to work in your life. To make it easier for you to remember them, just think of the acronym *ARRT:*

- A = Avoid
- R = Reduce
- R = Retain
- T = Transfer

Avoiding risk

Avoiding risk means exactly what it says: When none of the other strategies for treating a risk seems suitable, sometimes the wisest decision is to simply avoid the risk. For example, I avoid risks like skydiving, hang gliding, and auto racing. I'm sure I would enjoy those activities if I ever took them up. It's just that, for me, the rewards aren't worth the risks.

Here are some other examples where avoiding the risk may be the best strategy:

- Not licensing a teenage driver who is clearly still immature and irresponsible
- Not buying an expensive sports car while your driving record is poor and insurance costs are sky high
- Not buying a backyard trampoline for your kids because you can't prevent unsupervised use by other neighborhood children

Reducing risk

Reducing risk means taking actions that lower the probability of the loss happening at all or, if it does occur, lowering the loss's possible severity. If you've inherited Grandma's sterling silver, you can reduce the theft risk by installing a central home alarm and/or by hiding the silver well. If you have a valuable baseball card collection, you can greatly reduce the water damage risk by mounting and sealing the cards in waterproof plastic album pages.

Here are some other examples of ways you can reduce your risks:

- Regularly checking prongs on a valuable diamond ring to reduce the risk of loss of the stone
- Eating healthy foods and working out regularly, not smoking, and getting plenty of rest
- Not drinking and driving
- Buying cars that have safety features like air bags and antilock brakes and that test well in crash tests

Reducing risk has the advantage of being the one treatment strategy you can do the most with and have the most personal control over. It has other advantages, too. If you significantly reduce a risk:

- The risk may be small enough that you feel safe avoiding insurance altogether. For example, if you've stored your valuables in a safe-deposit box, you may not feel the need to insure them.

_____

_____

_____

- You may feel comfortable carrying higher deductibles. For example, you may be able to save 50 percent on your health insurance costs by buying a $2,000 deductible, and know that a high deductible is a smart choice because your healthy lifestyle results in few claims.
- You may be able to get insurance at a better cost.

Throughout this book, I talk a lot about reducing risk — and I recommend it as at least a part of the solution to managing many of the risks in your life.

Retaining risk

Retaining risk refers to the strategy of paying losses out of your own pocket. Retaining risk can be *voluntary* (such as carrying higher deductibles in order to lower your premiums). Retaining may mean choosing to take the entire risk on less valuable items; for example, you may forgo insurance on a $300 canoe. Retaining may mean not carrying insurance to cover low-frequency catastrophic losses that have almost no chance of happening where you live; for example, you probably won't buy earthquake insurance if you live in Minnesota.

_____

_____

_____

Retaining risk can also be *involuntary.* In this category are the surprises you get at claim time, the risks you take every day without even knowing it, such as the following:

- Not having any coverage to protect against an injury lawsuit from the person who delivers a package to your home-based business and falls and is injured on your icy sidewalk

- Not being protected against the lawsuit from your co-worker who was injured while riding with you in your company car

- Receiving only $30,000 for your $50,000 kitchen fire because of depreciation deductions under your home-owner's policy

- Being sued by a car-rental company for $10,000 in damages to a rental car — damages caused by a friend or co-worker — for which you naively agreed to be responsible when you scribbled your signature on the rental agreement

Much of the focus of this book is on uncovering these involuntary retentions — the many pitfalls of personal policies. Throughout this book, I expose these hidden risks and show you steps you can take to protect yourself.

_____

_____

_____

Transferring risk

Transferring risk refers to shifting the risk in whole or in part from yourself to another party. The most common form of transfer is the insurance mechanism whereby, in exchange for a predetermined premium payment, an insurance company will assume losses that you would've otherwise had to absorb yourself.

Here's an example: You transfer the risk of fire damage to your home to an insurer for $800 a year. Your home is destroyed by fire. The insurance company pays the entire cost to rebuild, the cost to replace all your destroyed belongings, and even the additional costs you incur to live elsewhere while your new home is being rebuilt.

The other type of transfer (the bad kind) occurs in just about every contract you sign in your daily life. "But I *never* sign contracts," you're thinking. I bet you do — everyone does. In any given year, you likely sign contracts for an apartment lease, a boat rental, a vacation condo, a rental car, a credit card, a real estate purchase, or a home-repair proposal. These are just some examples of the contracts you sign in your daily life. It's almost impossible to be alive and not sign contracts in today's busy world. In just about every one of these contracts, someone is trying to transfer some kind of risk to you, often without your knowledge. If there's a problem, you're simply out of luck. Courts don't accept failure to read what you've signed as an excuse.

Take a closer look at an everyday contract in which you assume responsibility unknowingly, and the surprises that can be waiting for you: wedding reception catering. You assume all liability for injuries to guests, even when they're caused by the negligence of the restaurant (for example, food poisoning). You agree to pay all defense costs of the restaurant in such injury lawsuits and to pay any judgment against the restaurant out of your own pocket.

Can you imagine how upset you'd be if some dear friends at your daughter's wedding reception suffered serious illness or even death from contaminated food, and you were forced to pay to defend the restaurant? Plus, you had to pay all judgments against the restaurant, just because you innocently signed a contract to do so?

Does this scare you? I hope so. Fear is a good thing when it keeps you from hurting yourself. And if you don't start paying attention to the routine contracts of your daily life, you could easily assume a risk that can ruin you financially.

_____

_____

_____

ARRT in Action: A Case Study

The four risk treatment strategies of avoid, reduce, retain, and transfer work together. In fact, you're more likely to combine the strategies instead of using them individually.

Here's a case study that's just one example of how you can put ARRT into action in your daily life: Let's say your son is about to turn 16, and he wants to get his driver's license.

You can obviously **avoid** the risks associated with a 16-year-old driver by not allowing him to get a driver's license. Avoiding is the strategy to take when none of the other strategies for treating a risk seems suitable. Odds are, when it comes to your teen, you'll be able to manage the risk through a combination of the other three strategies and allow him to drive.

You can **reduce** the risks of injuries, property damage, and lawsuits by

- Requiring your teen to spend 30 or 40 hours of practice behind the wheel, alongside you, while facing all different driving scenarios and weather conditions

- Buying your teen a structurally solid and mechanically safe car, with working seat belts and air bags, to minimize injuries

- Asking your teen to sign a contract in which he agrees
  not to drive after using drugs or alcohol, and you agree
  to pick him up anytime, anyplace, without giving him a
  hard time

You can **retain** some or all of the risk of damage to the car itself (collision, fire, theft) by either not buying damage insurance on the car at all or, if the car is worth too much, at least choosing large deductibles. This strategy will save you a bundle on your insurance costs.

You can **transfer** the ownership risk of personal lawsuits related to vehicle maintenance by transferring the vehicle title and maintenance responsibility to your teenager. This strategy won't absolve you of responsibility for your teen's behavior, but it can avoid lawsuits against you related to not maintaining the vehicle in a reasonable manner. Your teen has considerably fewer assets and income than you do and is much less a target for lawsuits than you are, so he'll need far less liability insurance coverage.

 Be sure to check your state law to find the minimum age at which your teen can legally own a vehicle; you can find this information by contacting your state's Department of Motor Vehicles.

3

Buying Insurance

A great insurance program has two key components:

- Your program is in balance in all major risk areas.
- Each policy that you buy is well designed with high limits for major loss coverages and with all the right endorsements that customize your policy to cover the risks in your life that would not otherwise be covered.

You'll have a better chance of accomplishing both goals if you take time to locate a highly skilled insurance agent who's an expert on every type of personal insurance that you need.

You want your costs to be competitive and manageable. But the true cost of your insurance program is not only what you pay upfront in premiums but, more importantly, what you have to pay out-of-pocket at claim time. Most people who shop for insurance put all the emphasis on the front-end costs — the premiums — and then may end up having to pay thousands or hundreds of thousands of dollars in uncovered claims later. When it comes to insurance costs, it's far better to pay a little too much in premiums than to pay for an uncovered major claim later.

What Makes a Balanced Insurance Program

You face several major risks regularly throughout your lifetime that, if they occur, can cause your financial ruin: major medical bills, major damage to or destruction of your residence, major lawsuits and the cost of defending them, long-term disability, premature death, and — especially for those over age 40 — the risk of extended long-term care.

Your insurance program is in balance if each of these major risk areas are equally well covered and you're not spending too much on one area and too little on another.

Many people have major-loss coverage that's out of balance. They may have a good medical plan with high limits but no coverage for long-term disabilities. They may have $1 million of life insurance on the breadwinner but none on the stay-at-home parent. Their home may be fully insured, but they have only $100,000 of coverage for lawsuits and no umbrella liability policy.

A highly skilled agent can help you identify imbalances in your insurance program and suggest the corrective action needed, which is why taking the time to find the right agent is important. Most people who buy insurance don't take the time to find the right agent for them. They let whoever answered the phone and gave them the quote be their agent, without any knowledge of that person's skill level. And they get a less-skilled agent than they could have had for the same price.

For more information on finding the right insurance agent, turn to the later section "Choose Your Professional Advisor."

_____

_____

_____

Customize Each Policy to Meet Your Needs

The ideal insurance policy is a single page that simply says, "If you have a loss — no matter what the cause and no matter how high the cost — we will cover it in full." No exclusions. No 20-page policies. Wouldn't that be wonderful?

Because that policy isn't going to be available anytime soon, you want to get as close as possible to that ideal using a combination of several policies. This book introduces you to the basics of each kind of personal policy and how to choose limits for each coverage. You discover what optional coverages everyone should buy and what optional endorsements are available to cover those risks unique to you that would not otherwise be covered under the basic policy.

One of the key guiding principles from Chapter 1 says, "Don't risk more than you can afford to lose." That means having all major risk areas in your life well covered. To accomplish that objective, you should work with a highly skilled professional agent.

_____

_____

_____

Choose Your Professional Advisor

Customizing a policy requires a great deal of coverage expertise and care. And that's why, for most people, locating and hiring the best possible advisor has to be the very highest priority when it comes to buying insurance.

How agents get paid

In almost all states, agents selling personal insurance get paid the same commission as every other agent representing that particular insurance company — usually about 10 percent to 15 percent — regardless of the agent's experience, the agent's skill level, or the quality of the insurance plan that the agent designs. This payment structure is both good news and bad news for you.

The good news: Getting an expert for the price of a novice

Although the flat commission compensation system is anti-consumer (rewarding quantity of sales rather than quality), you can really benefit from the system in one way: You can buy the very best talent for not a penny more than you would pay for the worst possible agent. The vast majority of the time, the person you talk with the first time you call a company will not be one of that insurance company's most skilled agents.

Almost all insurance buyers see an insurance premium as buying them one thing — an insurance policy. In reality, the premium pays for much more than that. The policy, the coverage, and the insurance company make up about 85 percent of the premium. Professional advice, policy service, and help from a professional agent when there is a problem make up the other 15 percent. Spend that 15 percent wisely, and get the best agent you can find.

The more complex your lifestyle and the more of a lawsuit target you are, the more important it is to take the time to find an agent with the most expertise that you can.

The bad news: Finding a needle in a haystack

The "everybody gets paid the same" rule for agent compensation has one big drawback: The marketplace pushes agents with greater skills away from smaller, personal insurance policies and their small commissions into business insurance, where the premiums and commissions more appropriately compensate the best agents' greater expertise. The current compensation arrangement makes finding agents with great personal insurance skills a difficult task.

Know what you want in an advisor

Okay, so you're sold on the idea of finding the best advisor that you can for the commission dollars that you're spending. Where do you look for candidates? And when you find two or more candidates, how can you select the one that's best for you?

You should build a checklist of what you want in your agent. Ask yourself the following questions:

- **Do I want my life, health, disability, long-term-care, and other coverages with the same agent?** You'll have the best-designed program if you can find one agent with the expertise to oversee your whole program — expertise in every kind of personal policy. At the very least, it's wise not to have more than two agents that you work with.

- **Is a regular, yearly review important to me?** If so, add this to your shopping list. A well-designed insurance plan starts to rust with coverage gaps if it's not polished up every year or two.

_____

_____

_____

- **Do I have a home business?** If so, you must find someone with small-business insurance expertise. Add that
  to your list.
- **Are top claim skills important to me?** Do you want the
  best possible claims coaching in order to maximize your
  claim when you file it? Do you want an agent skilled
  enough to fight successfully for your rights if your
  claim is unjustly denied or underpaid?

Then use the answers to these questions to screen potential
candidates.

Search for candidates

You're looking for an agent to probe your needs, identify coverage gaps, solve problems, help you resolve claim disputes,
do annual reviews, and, in short, provide greater expertise.
Here are some possible sources for candidates. Try to get at
least two to three prospects.

Word of mouth

Word of mouth is always one of the best sources when seeking
a professional of any kind. But be careful not to fall into the
price trap. Because so many people buy their insurance solely

on price, when you ask for a referral for a good agent, you may get: "Call Bob. He's a good guy. He saved me $200 a year." So you call Bob, get his quote, save your $200 or more, and end up with a good price for the wrong coverage. But you've done nothing about your uninsured coverage gaps.

To avoid the price trap, be specific when asking for a referral. You don't necessarily want the best salesperson. You want the person who will give you the best professional advice.

Professional societies

An insurance agent can earn a number of advanced insurance designations by completing a series of courses and passing the exams. Here are just a few:

- Chartered Property Casualty Underwriter (CPCU)
- Certified Insurance Counselor (CIC)
- Certified Life Underwriter (CLU)
- Accredited Advisor in Insurance (AAI)

Many others designations exist as well. Anyone earning any insurance designation has to spend 100 hours to 1,000 hours (for the CPCU) in the classroom and studying on her own, as well as pass national exams. These people have gained additional expertise in certain areas and have a commitment to

_____

_____

_____

professionalism and ethical behavior. Don't choose an agent based *solely* on her professional designations, but weigh these designations (or the lack thereof) heavily in your decision.

If you want some good leads to an agent prospect with expertise in personal property and liability policies — auto, home, umbrella, and so on — contact the following:

- **CPCU Society** (phone 800-932-2728; email `MemberResources@theinstitutes.org`; Web `www.cpcusociety.org`)

- **The National Alliance for Insurance Education and Research** (phone 800-633-2165; email `alliance@scic.com`; Web `www.scic.com`)

Insurance companies

If you already know you want to be insured with a particular company, go directly to that company for agent referrals. You can also go to the insurance company for agent leads if you've shopped ahead for a certain type of insurance and found one or two insurers that are the lowest priced. (***Note:*** All you know at this point is that they're the lowest priced for the coverage you shopped but not necessarily the coverage you need.)

What you need to find out from the insurer is who the company's best, most knowledgeable agents are. The insurance company knows who these agents are, but the company is unlikely, for legal and other reasons, to give you their names. So try this: Call the local company office and ask them to email you a list of all their agents in your state who have a CPCU or CIC designation. They may not have a list at their fingertips, but they can get it for you. This method should yield a small supply of quality prospects.

Make your choice

At this point, you've narrowed your choice to one or two candidates for your "job opening" for an advisor. You're probably thinking, "How do I, with limited knowledge, make this choice?"

Start by requesting a face-to-face meeting for the purpose of doing an insurance review for every policy that you have, including your group coverage at work. You'll be able to tell by your gut feeling whether this is the person for you.

If you've narrowed your field to two candidates, have both of them do the insurance review for you. The agent with the greater expertise and greater care for your well-being will stand out.

The job of protecting you from financial ruin caused by property or liability claims is an important one. Approach it as seriously as you'd approach choosing a doctor, lawyer, or accountant.

Don't get quotes at this stage yet. If you're comfortable and she has the expertise you're looking for, ask her to design a program for you with all the right coverages. Then have her quote what she recommends and meet with her a second time to review the quotes and get her help making choices. When all those changes are implemented, you should have satisfied both the components of a great insurance program.

When you've completed the reviews, ask about the agent's background, his educational and practical experience, and the kind of ongoing help you can expect — both in terms of regular fine-tuning of your program and in terms of the kind of assistance you'll get in a serious claim or dispute. Don't consider any candidate who doesn't offer you the big three:

_____

_____

_____

- The expertise to help you design a great protection plan with the fewest possible gaps
- Ongoing reviews and regular contact about new developments so your plan stays current
- Outstanding assistance at claim time, both coaching you and being a strong advocate for your rights in a dispute

Choose an Insurance Company

A good agent can advise you on both the financial strength and the quality of claim service of any insurance company that you're considering. If, however, you're buying direct without advice or you just want more information on a particular company, go to www.ambest.com.

A.M. Best analyzes and rates insurance companies based on their overall quality and financial strength. It gives insurers grades much like those in school — A++, A+, A, A−, B++, B+, B, and so on. The higher the rating, generally, the safer you are from the risk of the insurance company closing its doors and not being able to pay your claim.

Don't buy insurance from any company with an A.M. Best policyholder rating of less than A unless you have no other choice.

The larger your exposures and the greater your coverage limits, the stronger the insurance company rating you should seek. For example, if your income and/or assets make you a target for lawsuits, you'll probably buy an umbrella policy (see Chapter 6). The A.M. Best rating for that umbrella policy should, ideally, be an A+ or A++. Picking an insurance company can be a gamble. Fortunately, organizations like A.M. Best help improve your odds.

_____

_____

_____

4

Managing Your Personal Automobile Risks

Americans have a love affair with their cars, and because Americans own more cars per capita than any country in the world, a good place to begin examining insurance risks is to look at those associated with the ownership, maintenance, and use of our beloved cars. An automobile is one of the most dangerous devices you own. In one split second, driving a car can result in lawsuits, death, long-term disability, major medical expenses, and major property damage.

That's why it's important to spend time setting up a solid car insurance program that will keep you from suffering heavy financial losses following a serious car accident. This chapter shows you how to create a solid car insurance program.

Protect against Lawsuits

Your personal automobile is the single largest possible source of catastrophic lawsuits and legal judgments against you for major injuries, death, and property damage. This section fills you in on some specific strategies you can follow to protect yourself against this risk — first, by reducing your risk in the first place, and second, by buying liability coverage.

Reduce your lawsuit risks

You can reduce your risk of being sued by taking some non-insurance steps — steps that not only lower your risk but often lower your insurance costs as well:

- **Obey traffic laws, including the speed limit.** People who speed have many more accidents. A California study indicated that, with one speeding ticket in the last two years, your probability of having an at-fault accident increased 95 percent. With two tickets, your probability increased 170 percent. If you received three speeding tickets, you were 254 percent more likely to have an accident. If you have four speeding tickets, you're almost 300 percent more likely to have an accident. This should help you understand why insurance companies bump your rate up when you get speeding tickets.

- **Don't drink and drive.** Always use a designated driver. Period.

- **Perform regular safety maintenance on your vehicle.** Have your brakes, tires, steering, and lights checked by a mechanic.

- **When you're shopping for a car, buy a vehicle that's highly rated for low damageability and passenger safety.** Check out the Insurance Institute for Highway Safety Web site (`www.iihs.org/iihs/ratings`) for crash test results on various makes and models.

- **Opt for added safety features like air bags or antilock brakes.** They cost more, but they'll save you money on your insurance premium and reduce your risk of injury.

- **Always wear your seat belt and insist that your passengers do, too.**

_____

_____

_____

- **Buy child safety seats and always use them.** Look for a seat rated by the National Highway Traffic Safety Administration (NHTSA). For tips on child safety seats, go to www.nhtsa.gov.

- **Take a behind-the-wheel defensive driving class.** Even if you don't get a premium credit, you'll be a better driver and have less chance of being involved in a serious accident — either one that is not your fault or one that you cause. And fewer accidents means better rates (and maybe longer lives).

- **Require your teenager to have at least 30 hours of practice behind the wheel on his permit under all sorts of driving conditions before allowing him to get a driver's license.** No one can ever develop the skills needed to be a safe driver in just a few hours of mandatory driver's education.

- **Allow your teen to drive based on your determination of her ability to responsibly operate a car —** *regardless* **of when your state says she can legally drive.** A teen who behaves immaturely and irresponsibly out of a vehicle usually behaves immaturely and irresponsibly *in* a vehicle.

_____

_____

_____

Buy liability coverage

Liability insurance provides for your defense and pays legal judgments on your behalf. People who buy liability insurance frequently make two mistakes:

- **They buy far too little coverage.** "How much is enough liability insurance?" you may be asking. It depends on who the victim is. It also depends on how suable you are. I call this your *suability factor.*

- **They buy inconsistent limits.** For example, they have a $100,000 limit on their car, $300,000 on their home, and $50,000 on their boat. Suppose these are your limits and you injure someone seriously with your car. You have only $100,000 of coverage, yet had the same injury occurred at home, you would have $300,000 of coverage. See how illogical that is?

Your suability factor

Suability factor is the probability of an injured party suing you for large sums — often for more than the amount of liability insurance you're carrying. For that to happen, you must be worth something, either currently or in the future. Why? Because if there's nothing to go after, many attorneys won't take the case and help an injured party sue you.

Your suability factor is influenced by several elements:

- **Your current income:** The more you make, the higher your suability factor.

- **Your current assets:** If you have expensive cars and homes, lots of investments and savings, and other assets, your suability factor is higher.

- **Your future income:** If you're a medical intern, a law school student, or an MBA student, your suability factor is higher, even if you're currently living in a studio apartment and eating ramen noodles every night.

- **Your future assets:** If your parents are wealthy and you stand to inherit a lot, your suability factor is higher.

People with high current incomes or assets usually are aware of their suability. But people with little current income or assets often overlook their future income or asset potential and the effect it has on their current suability.

_____

_____

_____

If you have one or more of the elements of a high suability factor, you're more apt to be sued for amounts greater than your insurance coverage, and you need higher liability limits on *all* your insurance policies. An advantage of higher liability limits is that the closer your liability limit comes to the economic value of the injury you cause, the greater the likelihood that the injured party will settle for your insurance policy limit and not pursue you personally beyond that.

For some people, another variable in choosing a liability limit is their sense of moral responsibility. For example, a person who is not very suable may buy a higher liability limit than she would otherwise need in order to make sure that any fellow human being she injures is provided for financially.

The cost of higher liability limits

You may be wondering how much it costs to raise your liability coverage — well, it costs very little. Call your agent and find out for yourself — you'll be amazed. (Don't forget to raise all your liability limits on your other personal policies to the same limit as your car insurance.) Table 4-1 shows an example of fairly typical costs involved in raising liability coverage from

$100,000 for two cars, a home, a cabin, and a boat. (The numbers may vary depending on the insurance company and the circumstances of the insured.)

New Liability Limit	Additional Annual Premium
$300,000	$100
$500,000	$150
$1.5 million	$300
$2.5 million	$390
Each additional $ million	$90

Table 4-1: *The Cost of Raising Liability Limits from $100,000*

Coverage beyond $500,000 is sold in $1 million increments under a catastrophic excess policy commonly referred to as an umbrella policy. (See Chapter 6 for more on umbrella policies.)

When you look at what you're spending for the first $100,000 of coverage, you see that you can tremendously increase your catastrophic lawsuit coverage (not to mention your peace of mind) for just a little more money. Additional liability coverage is the best value in the insurance business.

The danger of split liability limits

Most liability coverage for homes, boats, recreational vehicles, and other personal policies is sold by insurance companies as a single limit (such as $300,000) that applies to all injuries and property damage you cause in a single accident, no matter how many people are injured or how much property is damaged. In other words, if you're in an accident, you have one pool of money to pay for *all* your liability.

Liability coverage for car accidents is also available as a single limit, but just as commonly it's sold with *split limits*. With split-limits auto liability coverage, you select three *limits* (the maximum your policy pays):

- One for injuries you cause to a single person
- One for all injuries you cause in a single accident involving two or more people
- One for all damage to property you cause in a single accident

Table 4-2 provides examples of three of the most typical combinations of split limits.

	Example 1	Example 2	Example 3
Injury limit per person	$50,000	$100,000	$250,000
Injury limit per accident	$100,000	$300,000	$500,000
Property damage limit per accident	$25,000	$50,000	$100,000

Table 4-2: *Typical Split-Limits Policies Sold*

If you buy a single liability limit of $300,000 on your home, cabin, and boat policies, you should get the same $300,000 limit on your car insurance. If you request that limit from an agent selling only split limits (instead of a single limit of $300,000), here are the split limits the agent may suggest as an alternative:

- $100,000 per person for injuries you cause
- $300,000 per accident for injuries
- $50,000 per accident for all property damage you cause

The danger of buying split-limits coverage is a false sense of security given to you by the injury limit *per accident*. The limit you're actually most likely to exhaust in a car accident is the injury limit *per person*.

Suppose you buy the limits shown in the second column in Table 4-2. Your policy limits you to $100,000 per person and $300,000 per accident for injuries you cause. Here are some hypothetical injury claims, what a jury may award, and what your policy pays with those split limits:

- You rear-end a car ahead of you with only one occupant, resulting in injuries to the driver's neck and back. Jury award: $250,000. You have a $300,000 limit per accident for injuries, so you're fine, right? Well, your limit per person that you injure is $100,000, so you're out $150,000.

- You rear-end the same car, but with two occupants. Both have neck and back injuries, one more serious than the other. Jury awards: $200,000 to one, $50,000 to the other. You guessed it. The policy pays the full $50,000 for the less seriously injured person but only $100,000 for the more seriously injured person, and you're out $100,000 ($200,000 minus the $100,000-per-person limit).

Neither of these scenarios involves catastrophic lawsuits, permanent serious injuries, or death. They are, in short, relatively ordinary. But look at what you would owe with split-limits coverage.

In both accident examples, the total amount of jury awards is within the $300,000-per-accident limit. But because the policy also has a per-person limit, the judgment costs you astronomical sums of money that you would not have owed if you had a $300,000 single-limit coverage.

Don't forget about legal fees, which in an accident defense case can run $50,000 or more. After you've used up your liability limit per accident, legal costs come out of your pocket.

_____

_____

_____

How can you avoid the per-person pitfall of split-limits coverage? Because the vast majority of car accidents involve cars occupied by one person, I recommend one of three strategies:

- **Select a per-person limit high enough to meet your lawsuit coverage needs for one person's injuries.**
  In the two earlier examples, for example, $250,000 to $500,000 of liability coverage per person would have saved you hundreds of thousands of dollars out of pocket for as little as $100 a year in additional insurance costs, if you're insuring two cars.

- **Buy *single-limit coverage* — one pool of money large enough to cover all injuries and property damage without a limit on the amount paid to any one person.** Because this includes property damage, and any amount spent to pay for property damage reduces the amount left to pay for injuries, be sure to buy a little extra coverage. The least amount of coverage you should consider is $300,000 to $500,000.

- **Buy a second layer of liability insurance, called an umbrella policy, of $1 million or more.** See Chapter 6.

Insure Your Personal Injuries

Injuries, often quite serious ones, happen in car accidents far more than in any other type of accident — plane, train, industrial, and so on. If you're injured in a car accident, you usually have more than one source from which to collect your medical bills and lost wages. One source may be your own health and disability insurance. Another source may be the personal liability coverage of the other driver, if the accident was his fault and if he has any insurance. But the process of collecting from the other driver can take months or even years. A third source is your car insurance.

You've got two types of coverage in a personal auto policy for your injuries in a car accident:

- Coverage for compensatory damages (what your injuries would be worth in a court, including compensation for pain and suffering) for your injuries caused by uninsured or under-insured motorists

- Coverage for your medical bills (and lost wages in some states) regardless of fault

_____

_____

_____

Uninsured and under-insured motorist coverage

When you're injured in a car accident caused by another driver, you can legally sue the other driver in most states to collect the fair value of your injury. If that driver has auto liability coverage, his policy pays you on his behalf, up to the liability policy limit he purchased. The economic value of your injury equals your out-of-pocket expenses plus compensation for your pain and suffering.

But what if the other driver has no insurance at all? Or what if the insurance limit he has is less than the costs of your injury? You can get a legal judgment against him and try to collect from him personally. But that can be an expensive, drawn-out process. Plus, if he's not worth very much and has a limited income, you may not collect much at all.

Fortunately, your own car insurance policy can solve the problem if you buy adequate limits of uninsured motorists and under-insured motorists coverage:

- **Uninsured motorists** are other drivers who are either unidentified (hit and run) or have no liability insurance.

• **Under-insured motorists** are other drivers who have some auto liability coverage but the economic value of your injury exceeds their liability limit.

I see these two coverages as a form of *reverse liability* in that you collect some or all of the economic value of your injuries caused by another driver from your own insurance company, almost as if they were the other driver's insurer. In short, uninsured and under-insured motorists coverages make up the gap between the other driver's liability coverage and the amount of liability coverage he would have needed to pay your claim in full — subject, of course, to the amount of uninsured or under-insured motorists coverage you buy.

How do the two coverages work? Say you're injured in a car accident caused by a driver who runs a stop sign. The economic value of your injury is $450,000. Now assume that you bought $500,000 of both uninsured and under-insured motorists coverage under your own auto policy. For an under-insured motorist, first, you collect for your injury from the other driver's insurance in the amount of the other driver's liability limit (say, $100,000). Then, you collect the balance of $350,000 from your own insurance company under your under-insured motorists coverage. Had the other driver been without *any* insurance, you would have collected all $450,000 under your uninsured motorists coverage.

Buy as much protection for your own injuries (caused by another person) as you buy to cover the injuries you cause to someone else. In other words, buy the same uninsured and under-insured motorists coverage limits as you buy liability insurance limits to the extent those coverages are available in your state. Why? You're worth every bit as much as a stranger you might injure. Cover yourself accordingly.

Save money on medical coverage

Coverage for your medical bills (and sometimes lost wages and *replacement services* — help around the home you have to hire) is generally offered by car insurance companies. Depending on your state's laws, this medical coverage generally falls into two categories:

- Medical payments coverage
- Personal injury protection coverage

Both coverages are similar in the sense that they pay your medical bills suffered in a car accident, regardless of fault, up to the limit you purchased. Personal injury protection has the added advantage (at a considerably greater cost) of also reimbursing you for some of your lost wages or replacement services. Some states even allow you (for an additional premium) to add together the personal injury coverage limits per car (called *stacking*) to cover a single injury (for example, $20,000 coverage per car multiplied by 3 cars on the policy equals $60,000 total medical coverage for a single injury).

Keep in mind three things when buying either coverage:

- **Check the law in your state.** State laws on medical payments coverage or personal injury protection coverage vary dramatically.

- **Buy only as much medical-related coverage as the law requires.** Medical and disability costs should be covered under other policies you have, so having additional car insurance coverage is redundant.

- **Don't buy additional coverage for your medical bills and/or lost wages from car accidents only.** This approach is betting that those particular kinds of expenses will happen just in an auto accident and is a violation of the principle "Don't buy Las Vegas insurance" (see Chapter 1).

Not buying more than minimum coverage limits for either medical payments or personal injury protection is an area where you can save money on your insurance. To fully transfer the risks of medical payments and personal injury, not just those arising from car accidents but from *any* illness or injury, you need major medical insurance and long-term disability insurance — both of which cover financial losses no matter how the losses are caused, rendering special insurance to cover the damages caused only by car accidents superfluous.

If you don't already have major medical and long-term disability coverage in your insurance portfolio, consider adding both immediately.

Insure against Damage to Your Vehicle

This section tells you how to manage the risks of damage to your vehicle, such as fire, theft, collision, vandalism, glass breakage, and so on. The ARRT non-insurance strategies from Chapter 2, particularly reducing and retaining, apply to managing vehicle damage risks. Here are just a few examples of how to use non-insurance strategies to reduce risks:

_____

_____

_____

- Carry an onboard fire extinguisher to reduce the risk of a serious fire.

- Always lock your car and install a burglar alarm to reduce the risk of theft.

- Park in a locked garage at home and always park in well-lit, non-isolated areas when you're away from home to reduce both theft and vandalism risks.

- Keep a safe distance behind the vehicle ahead of you to reduce the risks of both glass breakage and collisions.

You can use the retaining strategy by either choosing higher deductibles or not buying damage insurance at all and paying all claims out of your own pocket.

Insurance for vehicle damage is usually offered in two parts:

- **Collision:** Covers damage from colliding with another object (for example, a vehicle, post, or curb), regardless of fault

- **Comprehensive (also known as *other than collision*):** Covers most other kinds of accidental damage to the vehicle, such as fire, theft, vandalism, glass breakage, wind, or hail

_____

_____

_____

Both of these coverages are subject to a front-end copayment on your part, called a *deductible*. When buying either or both of these coverages, assume as much risk as you can afford, financially and emotionally, through higher deductibles — or don't purchase these coverages at all.

A couple of things to keep in mind here:

- **Make sure that the insurance company gives you enough of a price discount for taking the additional risk.** You find guidelines for choosing the most cost-effective deductibles, as well as for determining the point where dropping these coverages on an older car makes sense, later in this chapter.

- **If you're on a tight budget but still need higher liability insurance limits to protect future assets or income (like if you're a student in medical school), it may make sense to carry higher deductibles even if the money to cover them isn't currently available.** The savings will often pay for most or all of the cost of the additional liability coverage you need. The savings for raising your collision coverage deductible by $250 (from $250 to $500) is often enough to pay for an extra $200,000 of liability insurance. No matter how tight things are, coming up with another $250 to fix dents is easier than coming up with $200,000 to cover lawsuits.

If your driving record has deteriorated and your premiums are in danger of rising significantly with one more claim, I recommend very high deductibles, such as $1,000. In all likelihood you won't file a small claim — and risk higher rates — so why pay for something you're not going to use anyway?

Choose cost-effective deductibles

I estimate that the average person has a claim for damage to her vehicle every four or five years, so I advise my clients to choose a higher deductible if the *extra risk* (the difference in deductibles) can be recouped via premium savings within a reasonable time (in other words, four to five years). The number of years it takes to recoup that added risk is called the *payback period*. The payback period is the difference in deductibles divided by the difference in annual premiums.

If you're trying to figure out the most economical deductible, look at the hypothetical examples in Tables 4-3 through 4-6 to better understand how to determine the best deductible for you.

Table 4-3 is an example of insurance costs for collision and comprehensive coverage for a 3-year-old Lexus driven by a 47-year-old woman and used for business. Reading across from left to right in Table 4-3:

- The first row, "Deductible," shows the different deductible choices for both damage coverages.

- The second row, "Extra risk," shows the dollar amount of the difference between each deductible (the extra dollar amount you'll be at risk for if you choose a higher deductible).

- The third row, "Annual premiums," shows the annual insurance cost for each deductible.

- The fourth row, "Annual savings," shows the annual insurance cost savings if you choose the next higher deductible.

- The fifth row, "Payback period," represents the number of years it would take without a claim to save, through your reduced premiums, the amount of extra risk you would assume by opting for higher deductibles. The payback period is determined by dividing the extra deductible risk in the second row by the annual insurance premium savings in the fourth row. If the payback period is less than four or five years, choosing the higher deductible makes good sense.

	Collision	**Comprehensive**
Deductible	$250/$500/$1,000	$100/$250/$500
Extra risk (difference)	$250/$500	$150/$250
Annual premiums	$500/$400/$300	$250/$200/$150
Annual savings	$100/$100	$50/$50
Payback period (extra risk divided by savings)	2½ years/5 years	3 years/5 years

Table 4-3: *A 3-Year-Old Lexus Coupe, Driven by a 47-Year-Old Woman for Business*

In Table 4-3, the extra risk, from the second row, to increase the collision coverage deductible from $250 to $500 is $250. The annual premium savings, from the fourth row, to make that change is $100. Dividing the $250 extra risk by the $100 annual savings, you get 2½ years. That means if she goes 2½ years without any claims, she'll save $250 on her insurance costs — the amount of the added risk she took by raising her deductible. Using the rule of choosing a higher deductible if the payback period is less than four or five years, it's clear that raising the deductible makes sense.

The payback period from the example in Table 4-3 — even for the highest deductibles — is only five years for collision and comprehensive coverages, making it logical to take the added risk for both coverages.

Table 4-4 shows a 5-year-old Honda used to commute to work by a 35-year-old man. Although the premiums are less than they are for the more expensive Lexus in Table 4-3, the extra risk of the higher deductibles can still be recaptured in five years and is still worth taking.

Table 4-5 shows an older Chevy driven by a 19-year-old man with three recent speeding tickets whose rates are much higher due to both his age and his driving record.

Clearly, with payback periods of 2½ years or less for each deductible, this high-risk driver is better off with the highest deductibles possible. Not to mention that, with three tickets, he won't be turning in small claims anyway, because they may result in his being dropped by the insurance company. Would he be better off not carrying the coverages at all? See the next section for tips on making that call.

	Collision	Comprehensive
Deductible	$250/$500/$1,000	$100/$250/$500
Extra risk (difference)	$250/$500	$150/$250
Annual premiums	$300/$200/$100	$150/$100/$50
Annual savings	$100/$100	$50/$50
Payback period (extra risk divided by savings)	2½ years/5 years	3 years/5 years

Table 4-4: *A 5-Year-Old Honda Accord, Driven by a 35-Year-Old Man, 10 Miles Each Way to Work*

	Collision	Comprehensive
Deductible	$250/$500/$1,000	$100/$250/$500
Extra risk (difference)	$250/$500	$150/$250
Annual premiums	$1,200/$1,000/$800	$600/$450/$300
Annual savings	$200/$200	$150/$150
Payback period (extra risk divided by savings)	1¼ years/2½ years	1 year/1²/₃ years

Table 4-5: *A 12-Year-Old Chevy Cavalier, Driven by a 19-Year-Old Man with Three Speeding Tickets*

In Table 4-6, check out what happens to the insurance costs for this same Chevy if the 19-year-old sells the car to his 74-year-old grandmother who has never had a ticket in her life. The payback period for the highest deductibles far exceeds the four- to five-year guideline. This driver would clearly be better off with low to midrange deductibles.

	Collision	Comprehensive
Deductible	$250/$500/$1,000	$100/$250/$500
Extra risk (difference)	$250/$500	$150/$250
Annual premiums	$150/$100/$50	$75/$50/$30
Annual savings	$50/$50	$25/$20
Payback period (extra risk divided by savings)	5 years/10 years	6 years/12½ years

Table 4-6: *A 12-Year-Old Chevy Cavalier, Driven by a 74-Year-Old Widow with a Clear Record*

When to drop collision and comprehensive coverage

When deciding whether a vehicle's value has decreased enough to drop one or both of these vehicle damage coverages altogether, you apply the same four- to five-year payback guideline as explained in the preceding section. The only difference is that the extra risk you're assuming is the full value of the vehicle (less any salvage value collectible from a junkyard).

Assuming an old Chevy has a junk value of $300 and would cost $2,500 to replace with an equivalent automobile, the net risk is $2,200 (the $2,500 value less the $300 salvage value). Dividing the $2,200 risk by the collision and comprehensive premium will give you the payback period. Drop the coverage if the payback period is five years or less.

Road-Service and Car-Rental Coverages

Other coverages offered by most insurers are towing/road-service coverage and loss-of-use/car-rental coverage.

Towing/road-service coverage, though inexpensive, is better suited to automobile clubs, like AAA, Amoco, and others. They're good at it, claims are paperless, and they offer a number of other vehicle services — all for a flat fee.

On the other hand, towing/road-service coverage under car insurance is not paperless — you must pay the claim first yourself (usually), then file a formal claim report and wait two to three weeks for reimbursement. Coverage also is often limited to a dollar amount ($25, $50, and so on). A large number of these claims along with other tickets and accidents can impair your relationship with your car insurance company.

Loss-of-use/car-rental coverage is quite important. If a collision or other covered loss deprives you of your car, you probably need a substitute. If your car is badly damaged, or if there is a parts delay, that car-rental bill could be several hundred dollars out-of-pocket. Loss-of-use coverage covers the daily cost to rent a vehicle while yours is out of commission due to a covered loss. Costs covered typically range from $10 to $50 per day for up to 30 days. I recommend buying at least a $30-per-day benefit.

_____

_____

_____

There is another major benefit to loss-of-use coverage. Any delays by the claims adjuster in getting to your car penalize the insurance company — not you — by increasing the cost of the claim. So it's to the insurance company's advantage to see your car as quickly as possible. And the coverage saves you a lot of aggravation that repair delays would cause you otherwise.

5

The Basics of Homeowner's and Renter's Insurance

Homeowner's insurance policies are outstanding values — they offer tremendous amounts of coverage for very little money. But they're also, in my opinion, the most dangerous personal policies you can buy because they have the largest number of exclusions and limitations. When you're buying homeowner's insurance, you have to figure out which risks you're exposed to that fall outside the basic box of coverage. Then you can develop a strategy for dealing with those risks.

To buy the homeowner's insurance you need, first you have to understand something about the basic homeowner's policy. This chapter explains the fundamentals.

The Six Parts of a Homeowner's Policy

All homeowner's policies have six major coverage parts:

- **Coverage A:** Covers damage to or destruction of your residence. (*Note:* This coverage does not apply to renter's insurance policies.)

- **Coverage B:** Covers damage to or destruction of detached structures. (*Note:* This coverage does not apply to renter's insurance policies.)

- **Coverage C:** Covers damage to, destruction of, or theft of personal property anywhere in the world.

- **Coverage D:** Covers the added living costs you incur as a result of a loss covered by Coverage A, Coverage B, or Coverage C (such as lodging and meals).

- **Coverage E:** Covers non-vehicle personal liability for injuries and property damage at home and anywhere else in the world.

- **Coverage F:** Covers medical payments to guests injured on your premises, regardless of fault.

Note: When I refer to *homeowner's insurance,* I also mean renter's insurance (except for Coverage A and Coverage B, which don't apply to renters).

Coverage A

If you arrange the coverage on your residence properly, the insurance company fully repairs or replaces your home if it's damaged or destroyed by a covered cause of loss — such as a fire, a tornado, or whatever your policy happens to cover. If you insure your home for *less* than its full replacement cost, you need to be aware of two possible claims penalties:

- **The first penalty occurs if you are under-insured for a *total loss* (the complete destruction of your home).** Say your home — which you bought five years ago and insured for $275,000 — burns down. The cost to rebuild that house in today's market is $350,000. Because you insured the house for $275,000, you suffer an out-of-pocket loss of $75,000.

- **The second penalty for under-insurance occurs when your home is partially damaged.** Say you purchased a beautiful, 100-year-old, two-story home for $300,000 a

decade ago. You insure it for $250,000 — the purchase
price of $300,000 less the $50,000 lot value. Were you to
build this home new today, it would cost you $500,000.
Say you have a kitchen fire with extensive smoke and
water damage, and that the total cost to repair your
home is $150,000. Your insurance company pays you
$100,000. You're out $50,000. Why?

The vast majority of homeowner's policies will pay
the full cost to replace partial damage to your home
only if you insure your home for at least 80 percent
or more of the cost to rebuild new. If you insure your
home for less than 80 percent of the home's full replacement cost, your claim settlement will be depreciated.
On older homes, that may reduce your claim settlement by 35 percent or more. In this example, the cost
to completely rebuild your 100-year-old home isn't
the $250,000 you insured your home for, but $500,000.
Because $250,000 is far less than 80 percent of $500,000,
your settlement will be depreciated.

The policy essentially says that if you insure your
home for its depreciated market value (in this case,
$250,000), the insurance company settles with you on
a depreciated basis at claim time. The $50,000 penalty

in this example represents the amount of depreciation deducted from the repair costs.

If you insure your home for its cost to build new (or at least 80 percent of that value, according to the formula in the policy), the insurance company settles your claim for the full replacement cost of the damage — up to your policy limit.

Always insure for 100 percent of the estimated new replacement cost. Paying the extra premium is far easier than facing thousands of dollars in losses out-of-pocket at claim time from either not having enough insurance to rebuild if your home is destroyed or having your repair costs substantially depreciated on partial losses. Also, add a home replacement guarantee, if it's available. (See "Guaranteeing you'll have enough insurance to rebuild," later in this chapter, for more information.)

Coverage B

Virtually all homeowner's policies extend 10 percent of Coverage A — the residence coverage — to detached structures. In other words, if your home is insured for $200,000, you've got up to $20,000 worth of coverage for any detached structure — for no additional charge. Examples of detached structures include garages, pole barns, in-ground swimming pools, decks, and fences. (Always check your policy to see what's counted as a detached structure — policies vary.)

The Coverage B coverage for detached structure has two pitfalls:

- **The possibility of under-insurance:** If the structure can't be replaced for the 10 percent automatic coverage you get under Coverage A, and that's all the coverage you have, you could be left holding the bag. Make sure your detached structure limit equals the total replacement value of *all* detached structures on your premises.

- **The business exclusion:** Many insurance companies exclude any detached structure used even partially for business.

Here's an example from my own files that illustrates both pitfalls: Bob and Bobbie have a home insured for $150,000. They have a detached four-car garage with an upstairs loft. If they were to build this garage new today, it would cost them $35,000. They have automatic coverage from their homeowner's policy that covers their house in the amount of $15,000

(10 percent of $150,000). To be properly insured, they have to buy an additional $20,000 of detached-structure coverage (Coverage B) to bring their total coverage to $35,000.

In addition, Bob is self-employed — he owns and manages several rental properties. The detached garage, besides storing vehicles, also houses business equipment like lawn mowers, snowblowers, and so on. Plus, his business office is located upstairs in the loft portion of the detached garage.

What if a tornado destroys their $35,000 garage? Because they bought the extra $20,000 coverage, they do have $35,000 of insurance. The adjuster shows up with a $35,000 check the next day, right? Wrong. Because Bob stored business equipment in their garage, the insurance company could deny their *entire* claim.

This situation certainly doesn't seem fair, but it's how the coverage often works. The equipment had nothing to do with causing the destruction of the garage. Yet all the insurance company has to prove to deny the claim is that the garage was even *partially* used for business purposes.

If you have a detached structure on your home premises that is even remotely used for business other than for storing business vehicles, you must find out whether your policy has this business use exclusion. If so, be sure to request an endorsement to your homeowner's policy that permits that business use.

Coverage C

Two ways exist to value personal belongings for insurance purposes: *actual cash value* (used) and *replacement cost* (new).

Buy the replacement cost option. It's generally only about 10 percent more expensive, but you'll receive 30 percent to 40 percent more at claim time. If the total cost of replacing your belongings after a major loss is $100,000, with replacement cost coverage, you'll get $100,000 (minus your deductible). With actual cash value coverage, you'll probably get anywhere from $60,000 to $70,000, after deducting depreciation. At claim time you'll be glad you bought the better coverage.

One requirement of the replacement cost coverage is that you actually replace the damaged or stolen property. Until you replace it, the insurance company pays you only the depreciated value.

For residence owners, the basic homeowner's policy comes standard with personal property coverage of 50 percent to 75 percent of your Coverage A building limit. (The exact percentage varies, depending on the insurance company.) If you have a lot of high-end personal property, the automatic coverage provided under the homeowner's policy may not be enough.

Be sure you evaluate the contents-coverage limit on your policy and customize it to your needs. Don't just take what comes automatically with your policy — it may not be enough.

Coverage D

Your house is blown away by a tornado. You check into a motel and call your insurance agent. You'll need a place to live until you rebuild. You'll need to eat your meals out. But you won't have much in the way of utility bills. And you won't be buying any groceries. Some of your living expenses will go way up. Others will shrink. The difference between the two expenses — the *additional living expense* — is covered by Coverage D.

This helpful coverage pays the *additional* — not the total — expenses you have to incur for lodging, meals, utilities, and so on as a result of a covered loss (such as a fire, smoke, or a windstorm) that causes you to vacate your home. It usually will pay these costs for up to the policy limit, if any, or 12 months, whichever is exhausted first. With some insurers, the benefit is unlimited; with others, the benefit is a percentage of the Coverage A building limit.

Though higher limits are available, the odds of exhausting the base benefit are really slim, so almost no one buys more.

Coverage E

Though the cost of coverage for your personal liability for injuries and property damage that you cause represents a small part of your total homeowner's bill, in my opinion this is just about the most important coverage in the policy. Why? It covers lawsuits and the cost of defending against lawsuits, and it's so comprehensive, covering most of your non-vehicle personal liability worldwide.

Here are some examples of claims that Coverage E would cover, including some from my own files:

- Your 6-year-old spills red punch on the neighbor's white carpet, which requires a $3,000 carpet replacement.

- You get sued by a neighbor who, in spite of your repeated warnings, has allowed his child to climb your fence and harass your German shepherd. The child gets bitten, and you get sued.

- You're snowboarding and collide accidentally with a skier who sues for injuries.

The bottom line? Coverage E is great. Most homeowner's policies include the first $100,000 of coverage at no extra charge.

The two biggest mistakes I see people make with Coverage E is not buying more than the $100,000 of free coverage, and not setting their personal liability limits to match their other liability policy limits (on cars, cabins, boats, and so on).

You don't know where the lawsuit may come from, so you want the same amount of coverage protecting you no matter where it comes from. You wouldn't want different liability limits for different policies any more than you'd want different liability limits for different days of the week.

How much liability coverage should you buy? Here are some considerations:

- **Your suability factor:** How suable you are is affected by the size of your bank account, your income, your future income, and your asset prospects (in other words, inheritances). (See Chapter 4 for more on suability.)
- **Your comfort zone:** How high do you need the limits to go for your own peace of mind?

_____

_____

_____

- **Your sense of moral responsibility:** Many people with a modest income and few assets buy high liability limits to be sure that anyone they may hurt gets provided for.

The insurance cost of higher limits is minimal. Additional liability insurance is truly one of the best values in the insurance business. An extra $200,000 costs only about $15 a year; an extra $400,000, only about $25 a year.

So how much liability coverage should you buy? Choose a liability limit that considers your current and future assets and income, feels emotionally comfortable, satisfies your sense of moral responsibility to others, and matches what you would expect if you were the one suing. In my opinion, anyone with less than $500,000 liability coverage is under-insured. Most people should have limits of $1 million or more. Whatever limit you decide on, be sure to adjust your auto, boat, and personal liability limits to match.

Coverage F

The final (and least important) homeowner's coverage part is *not* health insurance for you or your family. Instead, it's what I call *good neighbor coverage.* If a guest gets hurt on your premises, even if the injury is caused by her own carelessness, this

_____

_____

_____

coverage pays her medical bills up to the coverage limit (usually $1,000).

You can increase the limit for an extra premium, but you should save your money. Odds are, most of the people you invite into your home have health insurance already. If they're seriously hurt and may sue, your personal liability coverage responds. Just be aware that you have this coverage if you have an injured guest.

Choose the Right Property Coverages

Coverages A, B, C, and D of homeowner's policies cover property damage to your dwelling, detached structures and their contents, and any increase in living expenses related to property damage. That's how homeowner's policies are similar.

How they differ is in the *kinds* of losses they cover. All homeowner's policies cover damage from fire or a windstorm, for example. But only some policies cover water damage from cracked plumbing or toilet overflows. And none automatically cover damage from a flood or an earthquake, though both coverages can be purchased. To choose the homeowner's policy best suited to your needs, you need to know which causes of loss are covered and which are not.

The causes-of-loss options

When you have a homeowner's claim for damage to your property, the first question is "Was the cause of the damage covered by the policy?" If "yes," your claim is paid. If "no," your claim is denied. Most insurance companies offer three choices for the types of losses covered:

- **Basic form causes of loss:** Very limited coverage. Limited to a handful of covered causes of loss, including fire, wind, vandalism, and very limited theft. This option is rarely sold or purchased anymore.

- **Broad form causes of loss:** Covers about 15 causes of loss. From my experience, the vast majority of the kinds of loss that damage a home or contents are covered. If you have a loss that's on the list, you're probably covered. If the cause of the loss isn't on the list, you're probably not covered.

- **Special form causes of loss:** The best. Covers any accidental cause of loss unless that cause of loss is specifically excluded. (Damage from floods, groundwater, sewer backup, earthquakes, and a few other causes of loss aren't covered.)

Here are some examples of losses *not* included in the broad form list that *are* covered by the special form:

- **Interior damage to ceilings and walls caused by melting ice and snow that backed up under the shingles:** Claims have averaged $4,000 to $10,000.

- **Scorched counters or floors from hot pans dropped onto them:** Claims to replace counters and floors run $5,000 or more.

- **Spills of any liquids on oriental rugs:** Claims to replace rugs range from $600 to $20,000.

The annual extra insurance cost for the special form over the broad form? Probably $75 a year.

Do *not* buy the basic form coverage — it's way too restrictive. I like broad form coverage because the majority of your losses will be covered. But my favorite is the special form because it puts you in the driver's seat — no matter how bizarre the cause, your loss is covered (unless it's specifically excluded).

The six most common policies

If you looked at a typical menu of homeowner's policies available from most insurance companies, you would see six entrees, ranging from light fare to a full-course meal. Each option is referred to as a *form*. One form is designed specifically for renters, one is specifically for town house or condominium owners, and the other four are for owners of private residences.

Table 5-1 shows the six homeowner's forms most commonly used in the industry, the type of buyer they're designed for, and the causes of loss covered under each (basic, broad, or special).

To choose the homeowner's form best for you, first determine what type of buyer you are — homeowner, renter, or town house/condominium owner. Then determine the causes of loss you want covered — basic, broad, or special — for the building and again for the contents.

_____

_____

_____

Type of Buyer	Form Number	Building Coverage	Contents Coverage
Homeowner	HO-1	Basic	Basic
Homeowner	HO-2	Broad	Broad
Homeowner	HO-3	Special	Broad*
Renter	HO-4	N/A	Broad*
Homeowner	HO-5	Special	Special
Town house or condo owner	HO-6	Broad*	Broad*

The special form is available as an option at an additional cost.

Table 5-1: *The Six Homeowner's Policy Forms*

For example, if you rent, you would choose Homeowner's Form 4 . It comes automatically with broad form coverage. You can buy the special form for an extra charge. If you're a homeowner and you want special form coverage on your structures but you're comfortable with broad form coverage on belongings, you would choose Homeowner's Form 3.

Which form do most insurers sell and 90 percent of homeowners buy? Homeowner's Form 3, covering buildings with the special form and contents with the broad form. The logic behind this decision is that the structure is the biggest property risk, and totally exposed to the elements, whereas most contents are more protected by being inside. It's a reasonable argument. I think Homeowner's Form 3 is a reasonable choice for most people.

 If you have expensive personal belongings, fine arts, expensive rugs, paintings, or antiques, or if you simply like having the best, special form contents coverage is the best choice for you. It's only about 10 percent more expensive than broad form coverage.

Here's how to get special form coverage for both your home and contents:

- **If you own a home,** you have two choices: Buy a Homeowner's Form 5, if available, or buy a Homeowner's Form 3 and add a special perils contents endorsement.

- **If you own a town house or condo,** buy Homeowner's Form 6, add a special perils endorsement to Coverage A (building coverage), and add a special perils contents endorsement.

- **If you rent,** buy Homeowner's Form 4 and add a special perils contents endorsement. (For more on insurance for renters, see the next section.)

_____

_____

_____

Renter's Insurance

People who buy renter's insurance do so when they don't own the structure they occupy, but they do own the personal property in the structure and they're concerned about that property being stolen. Specifically, they're concerned about their most prized possessions — their TV, stereo system, or customized bicycle. That fear of being ripped off is what draws many people to look into buying renter's insurance. And yes, if they are burglarized and have these valuables stolen, there will be coverage.

But renter's insurance is much more than just theft coverage. The policy has all the coverages of a full-fledged homeowner's policy, except for structural coverage. If you have a kitchen fire and, while your place is being restored, you have to live elsewhere, you'll have coverage for additional living expenses. If you cause that fire and damage the structure that you're renting, you're liable for that damage, and your liability coverage under the renter's insurance will pay for repairing that damage. The liability coverage also will defend you and pay any judgments against you for injuries to guests who fall on your newly waxed floor. And often overlooked is that that same renter's liability coverage applies anywhere else, too. For example, it will defend and pay any judgment against you caused by injuries you cause in sporting activities (racquetball, baseball, tennis, skiing, and so on).

Value your belongings

One of the mistakes most people make when they insure their belongings in a renters policy is to totally under-insure them. They buy $10,000 or $15,000 of coverage but can never replace everything they own for close to that amount.

I recommend that you use the 200 percent method for valuing personal property. Total up the replacement value of all your major items — furniture, appliances, television, stereo, and so on — and then double that number. You'll end up with an amount high enough to replace all your major possessions and still have an equal amount of money available to replace all your other possessions, such as clothing, dishes, silverware, towels, and other miscellaneous household items — items that are easy to overlook but that you'll still need to replace if something happens to them. That amount will also be high enough to replace bicycles, ski equipment, and other sporting gear, as well as tools.

_____

_____

_____

Buy the optional replacement cost coverage so that, in the event of a major loss, the insurance company will pay you enough to replace everything new. Otherwise, you'll be paid the depreciated value for your possessions — typically 40 percent less.

Evaluate your causes-of-loss options

Homeowner's Form 4, for renters, automatically includes a broad form causes-of-loss coverage (refer to Table 5-1), but, for a reasonable additional fee (typically less than $100 per year), you can change that form to a special form so that all losses are covered other than the exclusions. You should definitely consider this option if you have a lot of high-end furnishings or property you use away from home, such as customized bicycles.

Choose a liability limit

The standard renter's policy comes with $100,000 of personal liability coverage — not nearly enough to cover someone's serious injuries or loss of life that you cause. Here are two recommendations with regard to personal liability limits:

_____

_____

_____

- **Buy at least $300,000 and ideally $500,000 of coverage.** The cost is unbelievably cheap — typically $20 to $25 a year.

- **Buy the same liability coverage on your renter's policy as you buy for your car insurance liability.** Both liability limits are protecting the same assets and same income.

If you have a high income or the potential for a high income in the next few years, consider an umbrella policy (see Chapter 6).

Property Coverage Limits

Insuring your home and contents properly to get the very best payout at claim time means insuring both for their full replacement cost. You probably have a pretty good idea of the market value of your home, but where do you find the replacement value? And how do you compute the cost of all your belongings?

Determine your home's replacement cost

The *replacement cost* of your home is the cost to rebuild it. Most insurance companies estimate the replacement cost of your

_____

_____

_____

home using a computer program designed for that purpose. But how can you be sure their estimate is accurate?

Insuring your home for its replacement cost is important in order to avoid serious penalties at claim time. But you also don't want to spend more than you need to by over-insuring your home. The most accurate way to estimate your home's replacement cost is to spend $200 to $500 (or more) and have a professional appraisal done. But that strategy is tough on the budget, and it doesn't exactly follow the "Keep it simple" principle from Chapter 1.

Here are two strategies to cross-check your agent's estimate:

- **Double-check the agent's worksheet.** Have the agent send you her worksheet. Make sure all the features and square footage are correct.

- **Use your home mortgage appraisal.** If you've financed or refinanced your home recently, you paid for an appraisal and you're entitled to a copy of it. If you don't have a copy, call your mortgage company and request it. The appraisal is for market value, not cost new, but in almost all appraisals, the appraiser includes the appraiser's estimated replacement cost.

_____

_____

_____

Their numbers are typically conservative, so be sure your building insurance equals or exceeds the mortgage appraisal's replacement cost estimate. For example, if the insurance agent calculates the cost, new, of your home at $278,000 and your bank appraisal estimated it at $262,000, I'd be comfortable with the agent's number. But if your bank appraisal estimated the cost, new, at $175,000, I'd make an issue out of that big difference. If you send the agent your bank appraisal, I'll bet you can get her to adjust her number downward.

I've found that the larger and/or more customized your home is, especially if it's an older home, the more likely it is that the insurance company's estimate is wrong. Determining the replacement cost of your home is difficult but worth your time.

Guarantee you'll have enough insurance to rebuild

You've done your homework. You've double-checked your agent's replacement cost estimate and made appropriate coverage corrections. Suddenly, your home burns to the ground. You've insured your home for $258,000, but after the fire, the true cost to haul all the debris and rebuild is $292,000. You tried

_____

_____

_____

your best to buy the right coverage but your out-of-pocket loss is $34,000.

Good news: This problem has a great solution — an optional home replacement guarantee, usually called *extended replacement cost coverage.* Extended replacement cost coverage has three requirements you must comply with in order for the guarantee to be honored at claim time:

- You initially insure your home for 100 percent of its estimated replacement cost as determined by your agent or insurance company (with your input — see the preceding section).

- You agree to an inflation rider that annually adjusts your coverage limit by the construction cost index for new homes in your area and you pay the premium increase each year.

- You notify your insurer anytime you spend $5,000 or more in structural improvements and agree to the change in coverage and higher premium that results.

Many people forget about the third requirement, which voids their guarantee. However, spending $5,000 or more is reportable only if it makes your home more expensive to rebuild new. Examples of expenditures that do not void your guarantee are replacing worn-out items like roofs or heating and cooling equipment, or cosmetic changes to your home that increase your enjoyment and probably increase the market value but don't affect the replacement cost at all (such as stripping off wallpaper and repainting walls with contemporary colors).

Many insurers have capped their home replacement guarantee (usually 125 percent of your building coverage). Unlimited coverage, though, is still available. I like unlimited coverage, especially if you have an older home where the exact replacement cost is difficult to determine.

When insuring your home, always double-check the insurance agent's replacement cost estimate so you don't over-insure your home. And always buy the optional extended replacement cost coverage, without a cap if possible.

Estimate the cost to replace belongings

The most accurate way to determine the cost of replacing all your belongings is to take a full inventory of *everything* that you own. No one does that, but two methods can get you close enough.

The 200 percent method

I like this method and use it a lot because you can do it in 30 minutes or less:

_____

_____

_____

1. **Add up the estimated new cost for all the major items in your home — furniture, stereo, TVs, appliances, computers, and so on.**

2. **Double the total.**

   This ensures that you not only have enough coverage to replace all the major items you own but that you also have an equal amount available for all the smaller items.

3. **Add to that the values of any exceptional property or collections, artwork, tools, home workshops, and so on.**

 Keep it fast and simple. Use your best guess on values, or it won't get done.

The percent of building-value method (for homeowners only)

Oddly, the vast majority of homeowner's insurance buyers accept the amount of contents coverage that comes with their homeowner's policy (usually 70 percent of the building-coverage value). Why? Partly because it's easy, and partly because most people have no idea of the significant value of property they've accumulated over the years.

If you accept the percent of building-value method as a means of determining the amount of content coverage you have, make one modification. Inflate your contents limit by the value of any exceptional property: fine arts, antiques, tools, and so on.

Don't accept as gospel the estimates of others when they value your property, and don't automatically accept the stock coverage that comes with your policy.

Choose your deductible

The usual deductible that comes with a homeowner's policy is $250 per claim. Most insurers allow you to increase the deductible to $500, $1,000, or more, in exchange for a lower premium. When deciding how big a deductible to carry, use three criteria:

- How much can you comfortably afford, financially, out of cash reserves?

- How much can you emotionally afford? (If parting with that much of a deductible would bring on tears, it's too high!)

- How much premium credit are you receiving for taking the extra risk?

It's been my experience that the average home property claim typically occurs once every seven to ten years. My advice is to pick the deductible that has a seven- or eight-year *payback period*. Here's how to determine the payback period:

1. **Subtract the lower deductible from the higher deductible.**

2. **Subtract the lower premium from the higher premium.**

3. **Divide the number in Step 1 by the number in Step 2.**

   If the result is 8 or less (meaning that you'll recoup your added risk in eight years less), pick the higher deductible.

Document Your Claim

Suppose your house burns to the ground, along with every shred of your belongings. Without documentation, even great coverage won't get you an easy — or full — claim settlement.

Here are some easy ways of documenting your home and its contents:

- Take photos of the exterior of the house and any detached structures.

- Take photos of special structural features in the interior, like stone fireplaces, custom woodwork, and so on.

- Take a photographic inventory of all your personal property. Take pictures of every cupboard and closet with the drawers open. Don't forget storage areas, the basement, and property in garages and other structures.

- Keep your home blueprints, if you have any. They're wonderful for making sure you get exactly the house you had. (It wouldn't hurt to put a copy of your home appraisal and photos with the blueprints.)

 Having photos, blueprints, and other documentation won't help at all if they burn up in the fire. So be sure to keep them off premises.

6

The Personal Umbrella Policy

No one has enough liability insurance. In more than 2,000 insurance reviews for prospective clients, I've seen that at least 80 percent to 90 percent of them were grossly under-insured for injury lawsuits. The most common liability limits on auto and home policies I see are either $100,000 per person or $300,000 per accident. That's not enough to pay for all the medical expenses of the person you severely injure, plus a possible lifetime of lost wages and compensation for pain and suffering.

If you don't have nearly enough protection, what can you do? You can buy a second layer of liability coverage, called a *personal umbrella policy,* that sits on top of your other personal liability coverages for your car, home, and so on. It defends you and pays legal judgments against you when a covered lawsuit exceeds your primary liability insurance limits. Best of all, an umbrella policy is inexpensive — usually about $150 to $200 per year for $1 million of coverage, and about $75 to $100 per year for each additional $1 million of coverage.

Buying an umbrella policy includes some of the broadest coverage in the insurance business at an incredibly low price. Buying an umbrella policy also satisfies two guiding principles from Chapter 1: not risking more than you can afford to lose and not risking a lot for a little.

Affording an umbrella is easy. You don't even have to increase your insurance bill — just shift dollars away from less important coverages. For example, you can save a few hundred dollars by raising the deductible on your car insurance and homeowner's insurance by $500, or by dropping collision coverage on an older car. Those savings more than pay for an umbrella policy.

This chapter introduces you to the basics of umbrella policies, explains how one works with other insurance policies, and helps you determine how much coverage you need.

The Umbrella Policy's Major Coverage Advantages

With an umbrella policy, you gain more than just higher coverage limits for injuries and property damage you cause — although the higher limits are a great advantage. You also receive

- Additional coverage for defense costs when the defense coverage under your primary policies runs out
- Coverage for many types of lawsuits not covered by your other policies (coverage gaps)

Additional coverage to defend yourself

What actually happens when you're sued for a dollar amount greater than your primary liability insurance limits?

You receive, from your insurance company, a piece of mail like this:

We Care Mutual Insurance Company
Re: Your June 19, 2017 Accident
Dear Mr. Smith:
You are being sued by Mr. Jones, the injured party in the above-referenced accident, for $650,000. Your automobile liability insurance limit with us is only $250,000. We will pay your defense costs for the first $250,000 of this lawsuit. You will be responsible for your own defense costs beyond that amount.
We strongly suggest you hire your own attorney right now to protect you for that part of the lawsuit not covered by our policy.
Yours truly,
Corporate Attorney
We Care Mutual Insurance Company

Why do they send you this letter? Because each of your primary insurance policies defends you only for lawsuit amounts up to your liability policy limit. If you're sued for more than your liability limit, you're personally responsible for the amount of any lawsuit that exceeds your primary liability limit, including the cost of defense for that difference.

_____

_____

_____

Those added defense costs often run $75,000 or more. One huge advantage of an umbrella policy is that it pays for those added defense costs.

Gap coverage

My client Mike and several of his friends were all turning 50 at about the same time, so they decided to have a group party. They rented a big barn at an empty local fairground and decided to make beer and wine available, at no charge, which added a potential liability for alcohol-related car accidents.

Mike called me because the fairgrounds required the friends to carry $1 million of liability insurance for the one-day event that also had to include the fairgrounds as an insured party. I asked whether he was signing the rental contract personally. He said it was in the name of two of his friends. I advised Mike that a one-day, special-event policy would cost about $500. But I also advised him that if either of his friends had an umbrella policy, the friend might be covered automatically. Neither one did. Mike signed the contract because his umbrella policy fully covered him for $2 million of liability for this type of rental contract. His umbrella also was broad enough to automatically protect the fairgrounds, as he had contractually agreed

_____

_____

_____

to do, and to cover the risk of liability for alcohol-related car accidents.

The exposures that Mike faced were

- Liability for his own actions that caused injuries
- Liability he assumed in the contract, agreeing to be responsible for the actions of everyone else at the event
- Liability if any partygoer drank too much and caused an auto accident, resulting in a lawsuit — a lawsuit that any provider of alcoholic beverages at a social event may face
- The costs to defend and protect the fairgrounds for any lawsuit brought against it
- Liability for damage caused by anyone to the rented barn, such as a fire caused by a guest's thrown-away cigarette

Many of these risks were not covered by any other policy, at least not for the amount required by the fairgrounds. Mike's umbrella covered every single risk, automatically. His group saved the $500 cost of a one-day policy that may not have even covered all the risks in the preceding list. I sent the fairgrounds proof of insurance, and everybody was happy!

But one problem remained: On the remote chance that a lawsuit exceeded Mike's $2 million umbrella policy limit, by contract, Mike would have been solely responsible for that excess amount. Therefore, each of his fellow birthday celebrants separately signed a legal agreement to share equally in all losses not covered by the umbrella. By the way, the party was a great success!

The story illustrates a little-known, major advantage of a good umbrella policy. It not only provides a second layer of liability coverage on top of your other liability policies, but it also fills a lot of the gaps between the policies.

Coordinate an Umbrella with Your Other Insurance

The coverage under an umbrella policy can be triggered when you're sued for more than your primary liability limits. It also can be triggered when you're sued for something covered only by your umbrella and not by your primary policies (in other words, the gaps). When the latter happens, the umbrella "steps down" and defends and protects you as if it were primary coverage, subject only to a modest deductible, called a *self-insured retention* (SIR) — typically, $250 or $500.

In the fairgrounds story (see "Gap coverage," earlier in this chapter), the last four risks that Mike assumed were gaps and covered only by the umbrella policy. If any of those four risks occurred, Mike would have paid only the $500 SIR.

This section fills you in on how you might need to change your primary insurance to meet umbrella requirements and gives you tips for avoiding gaps between primary and umbrella coverage.

One reason that umbrella policies are so inexpensive is that they generally don't cover small lawsuits. An umbrella policy requires that your automobile, homeowner's, and other personal policy liability limits (also known as *primary liability limits*) meet certain minimum requirements. Depending on the insurance company, the minimums vary from about $100,000 to $500,000. To get an umbrella, you must first raise your primary liability limits to these minimums and guarantee that you'll always maintain them. If you violate this guarantee and fail to meet these minimum requirements, you'll be personally liable for the difference between what you've guaranteed your coverages will be and what they actually are.

_____

_____

_____

Say that the minimum auto liability coverage needed to obtain the umbrella you have is $500,000, but your coverage has slipped to $250,000. If you're found liable for $700,000 in damages, the umbrella policy still kicks in after the first $500,000 has been paid — $250,000 by your auto insurance company, and $250,000 by you. (You promised to maintain $500,000 of coverage. You broke that promise by carrying only $250,000. You owe out of your own pocket the $250,000 shortfall.)

Insurance companies offering umbrella policies are not consistent in the amount of primary liability coverage that they require. Talk to your agent to be sure that your primary coverage always meets your umbrella requirements.

You must be aware of very serious dangers:

- **Don't let any primary policy cancel for nonpayment.** If you do and you're sued, you'll have to pay the loss out-of-pocket, which otherwise would have been covered.

- **Pay attention to all notices from your umbrella insurer.** They often require you to raise one or more of your primary coverage limits as a condition of keeping the umbrella. If you don't raise your limits as required, you'll be personally responsible for the gap.

_____

_____

_____

Determine How Much to Buy

The bottom line: Buy $1 million more umbrella coverage than you think you need. If you think you don't need an umbrella at all, buy a policy with $1 million of coverage; if $1 million sounds right, buy a $2 million policy; and so on.

Most people underestimate the economic value of a serious injury, as determined by a court of law. Also, an extra million dollars of coverage costs so little — around $75 a year. When it comes to catastrophic lawsuits, you're better off erring on the high side. No one ever went bankrupt over a $75 premium.

Review available limits

Personal umbrella policies are sold in million-dollar increments. Most insurers offer a maximum available coverage limit from $2 million to $5 million — several up to $10 million. Beyond $10 million, the choices are limited and the cost per million escalates because those buying more than $10 million of umbrella coverage are generally quite wealthy and highly vulnerable to lawsuits.

Assess how likely you are to be sued

In addition to the seriousness of an injury, several factors influence not only the likelihood of your being sued for more than the amount your policy covers you for, but also the dollar amount of the lawsuit.

Your current financial status factor

The size of your current income and/or current assets, particularly liquid assets like investments, affects the probability of your being sued for an amount that's greater than your automobile or homeowner's liability limits. If you have a high income and/or a high net worth, you're very suable.

I often see people who have only one of the two — a high income or a high net worth — overlooking how suable they really are. People like new doctors or lawyers in their first year of practice, making almost six figures, but with no money in the bank — yet. Or seniors on a modest retirement income but with a large, mostly liquid, portfolio. Both types of people are highly suable and definitely should have an umbrella policy — probably with limits of $2 million or more.

_____

_____

_____

Your future financial status factor

If you get a large judgment against you today, for more than your liability insurance limits, it sits out there in limbo waiting for your financial situation to improve. Most people easily overlook their future suability when they're assessing their need for an umbrella policy. If you're a medical student, a law student, a computer engineer — anyone training for a high-paying career — keep this in mind. If you think you may have a lot more money in the future than you have today, you need an umbrella policy to cover your liability risks.

The exceptional risk factor

Lawsuits can occur from either activities (like hunting, fishing, or playing sports) or exposures (like cars, homes, and animals). The exceptional risk factor recognizes that one or more of the activities or exposures in your life has a greater potential of causing serious injuries or death and, thus, more substantial lawsuits. Examples include owning a pit bull, operating a day-care center, and having a swimming pool (especially with a diving board). If you have these or other exceptional risks that have large lawsuit potential, you're a candidate for an umbrella, even if you're of modest means.

_____

_____

_____

The legal environment factor

The legal climate in your geographic area is definitely a factor in the size of legal judgments and jury awards. In California, where there are a zillion lawsuits for substantial amounts of money, you need a larger umbrella policy limit. In rural Arkansas, where lawsuits are rare, you may still need an umbrella, but the legal environment is probably not a factor in how large it needs to be.

Your personal comfort factor

Insurance is all about peace of mind. When you decide on an umbrella policy limit, do a gut check. If you still feel fearful of possibly not having enough insurance, spend an extra $75 and buy another $1 million of coverage.

Your moral responsibility factor

Sometimes clients remind me of that golden rule about caring for your fellow humans. They're often of modest means and not necessarily very suable. They may not really need an umbrella. I'll suggest a liability limit on their automobile, homeowner's, and other policies — say, $300,000 — and they'll say, "Oh, no, I want more than that. If I seriously hurt someone,

I want to make sure he's fully cared for. I can't undo the hurt I've caused in his life. But at least I can help take care of his financial burden." Such people are rare and wonderful.

Bottom-line recommendations

So you've considered all the factors that go into deciding to buy an umbrella policy, and now you just want a dollar figure. Here are my recommendations for umbrella policies:

- Buy a personal umbrella policy of at least $1 million.
- Buy at least $2 million in coverage if you have some affluence.
- Buy at least $5 to $10 million in coverage, or more, if you're very affluent.
- Buy $1 million more than you think you need.
- Buy a policy that covers the major liability gaps in your primary insurance program.

7

Making the Best Group Health Insurance Decisions

The good news about group health insurance is that some-body else is paying part of the premium. The bad news is that your plan choices are somewhat restricted, and the coverage stays with the job when you leave. This chapter helps you make good choices about group health insurance while you're employed and offers recommendations about continuing your coverage after you leave.

Pick the Best Group Health Insurance

Having to make group health insurance decisions can be difficult. There's no agent in your corner who can coach you. The insurance company or your employer can answer questions, but they can't give advice. Without good information, it's easy to make a serious mistake.

These are just a few of the kinds of questions I get from my clients about their group health insurance programs:

- Should I cover my spouse under my group insurance even though she's covered on her own policy at her job?

- How can I, as a single parent, avoid paying for a nonexistent spouse under the group family rate?

- Should I insure my college daughter on my group plan if she buys the school health insurance coverage?

- I have three different group plans to choose from at work. Which is best for me?

The following sections give you some tips on making good decisions on these and other issues.

Choose between two or more plans

I often get calls from clients who want help choosing among group insurance options offered to them at work. Having multiple options is especially common with large employers or the government. If your employer offers more than one group health insurance option, do the following:

- **Consider price last.** The only exception to this rule is if your finances are in poor condition. Otherwise, set aside cost for now.

- **Look at the five ingredients of a good health insurance plan and see how the insurance options you have to choose from compare.** They are a coverage limit high enough that it won't likely ever be exhausted, even for the most catastrophic medical expenses; an annual dollar limit you can live with on your out-of-pocket maximum (the *out-of-pocket maximum* limits your annual responsibility for your health insurance policy co-payments and deductibles); no dollar limits on types of expenses, such as dollar limits on daily room charges or dollar limits for types of surgical procedures; freedom to see specialists without a referral; and worldwide coverage.

_____

_____

_____

With any luck, at least one of the available plans includes all five ingredients. If it does, take that one. If two or more plans include all five ingredients, choose the one that also has paperless claims (meaning the doctors and hospitals file the claims directly to the insurance company). If two or more plans also offer paperless claims, then, and only then, decide on price.

Suppose your employer offers these three choices for group health plans for your family of four:

- Option A is a true freedom-of-choice plan where you can go anywhere you want for care. The only drawback is that you have to file your own claims. Your monthly cost is $750.

- Option B is a limited-choice managed-care plan. It meets only one of the five key criteria of a good plan — it has a limit on annual out-of-pocket expenses. Its only advantage is low cost — $475 per month.

- Option C is a hybrid of A and B. You can get care anywhere without a referral. Its only drawback is that if you go outside the rather substantial primary-care network (86 percent of the doctors in the state), you'll face a $300 deductible and probably will have to file your own claims. Your cost is $650 per month.

If these were your choices, you'd choose Option B only if, due to poor finances, price was all-important. It meets only one of the five criteria of a good plan.

You'd choose Option A if access to any doctor anywhere was worth the extra $1,200 a year (over Option C) and you could stand to file your own claims.

Personally, I would choose Option C. (In fact, these were my choices, and I did choose C.) It meets all five criteria of a good plan, and claims are paperless. I'm comfortable with the doctors who are available to me, and I can actually go to any other doctor if I'm okay with higher co-pays and filing my own claims.

To help you make a good decision, if you're still unclear about what choice to make, consider spending $100 to $200 to consult with a good insurance agent you know who is an expert on health insurance — maybe the agent who helped you with your life insurance. Bring in your group insurance options. You shouldn't need to buy more than one hour of the agent's time.

Cover your spouse and dependents

The following list includes some of the issues I'm asked about regarding how best to cover family members, along with my recommendations:

- **Double-covering a spouse:** The question of whether to cover a spouse under your plan as well as under your spouse's plan comes up most often when each spouse has coverage paid entirely by the employer and one of the two employers also pays all or most of the spouse's and dependents' coverage.

  Don't double-cover yourself or your spouse. When two companies insure the same person, you can't collect twice, so claims are shared or fought over. It becomes a claims nightmare. Instead, choose the plan that best meets the five criteria of a good health insurance plan.

- **Covering children when both spouses have a group plan:** Where should you cover the children — under your plan or your spouse's? In this situation, you weigh out-of-pocket costs in premiums, co-payments, and deductibles against the coverage of each plan.

_____

_____

_____

These out-of-pocket costs can be dramatically different. But again, choose the plan that best covers the five criteria. Price should be the least important part of the decision.

When choosing which plan is best, don't minimize how important the ability to choose top specialists will be if one of your precious ones is facing a serious illness or injury.

- **Avoiding the single-parent penalty:** The most equitable group plans charge a price per head. So if you're a single parent, you don't pay for a nonexistent spouse. Or if you're childless, you don't pay for nonexistent children. But it doesn't always work that way. Sometimes group insurance offers only two choices — individual and family. Family includes two spouses and all children for one price. But family also includes single-parent families and childless families. If your family is small, you pay the same amount as a person with a very large family.

Here's how you can avoid paying for nonexistent family members, assuming that your dependents are in good health. Accept the group coverage on yourself because the employer is footing at least part of the cost. Buy a quality individual policy for your dependents. If even one of your dependents has a health problem that would make him ineligible for individual coverage, bite the bullet and pay the family rate at work to get your dependent covered.

Continue Coverage When You Leave Your Job

Since 1985, the federal government has taken steps to allow employees and dependents to continue their health insurance when they would otherwise have lost it due to terminated employment, divorce, or other life events. The government's goal has been to try to make group health insurance portable, especially for those whose medical history would not allow them to qualify for individual health policies.

_____

_____

_____

This section fills you in on two federal laws that may give you some insurance continuation rights when you lose your group health coverage, and it offers advice on when to exercise those rights.

COBRA

The Consolidated Omnibus Budget Reconciliation Act (COBRA) gives employees of companies that employ 20 or more people the right to continue group medical coverage at their expense when their coverage under an employer's plan ends, for a period of time — usually 18 months or 36 months.

Generally, COBRA applies only to employers with 20 or more employees. But several states have enacted laws requiring COBRA to apply to smaller employers, too. Check with your state insurance department, or click on your state on the National Association of Insurance Commissioners website (www.naic.org/state_web_map.htm) to see the laws where you live.

What triggers eligibility

You're eligible for COBRA if any of the following occur:

- Your employment ends for any reason other than gross misconduct.
- You, as a covered spouse, and the covered employee get divorced or legally separated.
- Your hours are reduced below the minimum necessary to qualify for group coverage.
- You become eligible for Medicare.
- You become totally disabled.
- You cannot continue your children's coverage after their age disqualifies them from continuing under your group plan.
- The covered employee dies, if you're the spouse or child of the employee.

Your rights when a COBRA event is triggered

You've lost your job. Your health coverage is ending on the last day of this month. Your boss has handed you a form to sign with your decision on whether you want to continue your health insurance under the company's group policy. You're wondering, "Do I have to decide right away? How long do I have to make payments if I do elect COBRA?"

Here are some answers to those and other questions:

- **Required notices:** Your employer must notify you of your COBRA rights in writing when you're first hired and at the time of a triggering event. And when the triggering event happens, you have 60 days from the *later* of the day the notice was sent to you or the day your group health coverage ends to elect your COBRA continuation option.

- **Payment of premiums:** You have 45 days from the date you officially elect to continue your group coverage to pay the employer the first premium. You must pay retroactively back to the date your group coverage ended. So if your group coverage ended on June 30 and you elect to continue under COBRA on August 29, you have until approximately mid-October before the first premium is due. But if the premium is $700 a month for your family, you would need to remit $2,800 for July, August, September, and October, plus another $700 by October 31.

_____

_____

_____

After you've elected the coverage, all future monthly premiums for each month are due by the first of that month, although, by law, you can be up to 30 days late and not lose your coverage.

The employer is not required to, and generally will not, bill you. So if you forget to send a payment within 30 days of the due date, you're uninsured retroactively on the due date and you lose all further COBRA continuation rights.

If you know that you'll need the coverage for only a short time (for example, you're eligible for coverage from your new employer in 120 days), eliminate the risk of accidentally missing a payment due date. Pay your ex-employer the full four months of premium payments in advance.

- **Termination:** COBRA continuation coverage ends in the following situations: You voluntarily terminate it; premiums aren't paid within 30 days of the monthly due date; a covered person becomes covered under another plan; a covered person becomes covered by Medicare; the employer discontinues offering group health insurance to all employees; the COBRA continuation maximum period has ended.

To find out more about COBRA rights in your state, check with your state insurance department.

Make your COBRA election decision

If you're not sure whether to exercise your COBRA rights, here are a few general guidelines to help you with your decision:

- **Don't go even a day without major medical insurance.** Remember the rule from Chapter 1: Don't risk more than you can afford to lose.

- **Don't use temporary health insurance when you're between jobs if you qualify for COBRA.** Always exercise your COBRA continuation option instead. Yes, it's more costly, but unlike temporary policies, it covers pre-existing conditions.

- **Do exercise your COBRA continuation options anytime your maximum possible need for coverage won't exceed the maximum period of your COBRA option.** The COBRA option is seamless, and it allows you to continue using the same doctors in the transition period.

- **If the maximum possible need for coverage exceeds the length of your COBRA options, do continue COBRA for the short term while applying for individual coverage.** Then drop the COBRA option when the individual policy is approved and all preexisting conditions are fully covered.

HIPAA

The goal of the Health Insurance Portability and Accountability Act of 1996 (HIPAA) is to make it possible for you to move from one job to another when you or family members have health problems that otherwise would keep you trapped in your current job because either you would be turned down for health insurance at a new job or your preexisting medical problems would be excluded.

HIPAA rules also entitle a person losing group insurance at an employer, after COBRA options expire, to apply for individual coverage with no preexisting condition exclusion if they meet certain conditions.

A *preexisting condition* generally means any physical or mental health problem diagnosed, cared for, or treated in the six months prior to the enrollment date on your new group plan.

The HIPAA law makes it possible for you to change jobs even if you have a preexisting medical condition by

- Requiring that all insurers of groups of two or more employees cannot decline coverage on a new applicant for group insurance solely for health reasons.

- Limiting the length of time a preexisting condition can apply to a newly hired employee to 12 months (18 months for late entrants).

- Giving credit for any prior group or individual coverage during the 12 months prior to the effective date of the new group coverage. (For example, if you had coverage for 9 of the past 12 months, you would have only a 3-month exclusion on preexisting conditions.)

- Banning pregnancy and prenatal problems from being considered preexisting conditions.

Be sure to check for the most current information on HIPAA before acting. Laws can and do change.

HIPAA rules apply to any application for group health insurance offered by a company that has two or more employees. It also applies to applications for individual health insurance plans but only if your prior coverage was group coverage.

_____

_____

_____

HIPAA rules don't apply to changes from one individual health policy to another individual or group health policy. You can still be declined because of preexisting problems or have preexisting health problems excluded from the coverage. Therefore, don't ever drop an existing individual plan for another individual plan if you have preexisting conditions that won't be covered under the new plan.

Whenever individual or group health coverage you have is terminated (by you or by the employer), HIPAA rules require that the insurer provide you with a *certificate of credible coverage*. Give the certificate to your employer when you start your new job, and apply for the new company's group coverage. Likewise, give the certificate to your health insurer when you apply for an individual policy. As long as you've had health coverage for at least 12 months, with no lapse of 63 days or more, you can't be turned down for coverage or be subject to any unique limitations on account of preexisting conditions.

8

Managing the Risk of Long-Term Disability

When you're building your insurance program, you need to deal with five possible causes of a *major* financial loss through insurance:

- Lawsuits
- Destruction of home and personal property
- Major medical bills
- Premature death with dependents
- Long-term disability

Most people carry protection for the first four threats, but they don't protect themselves from long-term loss of income from illness or injury unless their employer provides the insurance. Yet, before age 65, a person is three times more likely to become disabled for six months or more than to die.

Adding to the seriousness of the situation, the economic loss to disability survivors is greater than it is for families after the death of a loved one; not only is the income lost, but the disabled person still needs a roof over her head, still has ongoing living expenses (such as groceries, utilities, and mortgage payments), and often needs additional care. Without this critical coverage in your insurance program, you're risking a major financial crisis — and it doesn't have to be this way.

This chapter explains how best to plug this serious gap in protection.

Decide Whether to Buy Long-Term Disability Insurance

Chapter 1 introduces you to seven tried-and-true principles to help you make good insurance buying decisions. Here are three of them that you can apply to the decision as to whether you need long-term disability insurance:

- **Don't risk more than you can afford to lose.** Ask yourself if your paycheck stopped today, and you didn't have it for the next five or ten years, what would your life be like? How would that impact your making the mortgage payment? Putting food on the table? Your family's peace of mind and stress level? If you don't have another source to replace that lost income, you need to have long-term disability insurance.

- **Consider the odds.** Just how likely is a long-term disability? Pretty likely regardless of your age.

  One out of three people in the workforce today will be disabled three months or more before age 65. One out of seven will be disabled for *life*. If you're disabled for as long as one year, your chances of being disabled for a long time are staggeringly high. In fact, you have a 40 percent chance of being disabled more than five years. If you're 25 years old and an injury or illness knocks you out of work for just three months, you have a one in four chance of having that disability last for life. That could be 40 years or more.

Clearly, the odds of a long-term disability causing you severe financial hardship are way too high to ignore.

- **Don't risk a lot for a little.** If the risk is great and the insurance cost is relatively small in relation to the risk, you should buy the insurance. Just how expensive is long-term disability insurance? On average, the cost runs 2 percent to 3 percent of your taxable income. If you don't have long-term disability insurance right now, you're definitely risking a lot for a little.

The risk of disability is real. And when it happens, it can last a long time. Protecting yourself from this huge financial risk with a good long-term disability insurance policy won't cost you much. *Remember:* The only thing worse than a long-term disability is a long-term disability with no income.

Determine How Much Insurance You Need

The goal of a good long-term disability strategy is to provide you with enough personal and insurance resources that you won't have to make major life changes (such as selling your home) if a disability occurs. Being disabled is traumatic enough without having the added pain and stress of big changes in your lifestyle.

Having the right amount of coverage is crucial. Too little coverage may mean that you still have to make major life changes in the aftermath of a disabling injury. Too much coverage and you're spending money unnecessarily.

To figure out how much disability insurance you need, you have to determine how much money you need every month to pay the bills. You have two ways to determine your monthly income need:

- **The hard way:** The hard way is to make up a budget of your monthly expenses from memory. Not only is that method extremely time consuming, but I've found, through working with scores of clients over the years, that it's also very inaccurate. People tend to underestimate their actual needs by about 20 percent.

- **The easy way:** The easy way is the approach I recommend. The computation can be accomplished in about 20 minutes and is extremely accurate. Just grab your last three months' statements for your personal checking account(s). On the top of page one of each statement, you see a figure for the total amount of checks written for that month. Add the totals for each of the three months and divide by 3 to come up with a monthly average income need. If any particular month is extremely distorted — because you took an expensive vacation, for example, or were paying for holiday gifts — use a different month. Whatever number you come up with, add 10 percent to 20 percent (because expenses normally *increase* during a disability).

Insurance companies limit how much coverage you can buy to about 80 percent to 90 percent of your take-home pay. You may not be able to buy as much as you'd like to have. If this happens, take their maximum and make sure you have a purchase option included so that, as your income grows, your coverage can, too.

The Special Lingo of Disability Insurance

Disability insurance policies have their own unique terminology, using language you won't find in any other insurance policy. You need to understand these terms to make a good decision on those policy features that are important to you.

Total disability

A person is considered totally disabled if he is unable to perform *all* the principal duties of his job, or any other job for which he's reasonably suited, considering his income, education, and experience. The pitfall to be wary of here is that if you can work only a few hours a week, you would have zero coverage under a policy covering only total disability.

Residual disability

Residual disability usually means proportionate coverage when you're unable to work full-time (from a back injury or a heart attack, for example) and usually resulting in an income loss of at least 20 percent. Under policies that cover only total disabilities, you would not receive a dime in benefits. But with residual coverage, if you work part time and earn 40 percent of your predisability income, you'll receive 60 percent of your monthly benefit.

I strongly recommend this coverage for absolutely everyone. Be sure to add a residual disability coverage option to any disability policy you buy. Without it, you won't get paid a disability insurance payment if you can still work even one or two days a week.

Make sure that the residual benefit period isn't limited. If your disability coverage goes to age 65, so should the residual coverage. (Many benefits last only six months.)

Elimination period

The term *elimination period* is disability lingo for *deductible*. The elimination period or waiting period represents the number of months you're willing to wait, while disabled, before coverage begins. Usually you have a choice of 30, 60, 90, or 180 days. Your choice will depend on how much money you have in the bank as a safety net combined with how long your employer will continue your salary or provide sick leave following a disability.

The longer you can wait, the lower your premium will be. For example, waiting 60 days typically gives you about a 30 percent savings compared with a 30-day elimination period. Waiting 90 days saves you about another 10 percent. Premiums continue to go down as you increase the elimination period beyond three months, but by much smaller amounts. Your best bet is usually either a 60-day or 90-day elimination period.

 Because there are always delays in getting a claim check, if you're trying to decide between two elimination periods, choose the shorter of the two. For example, if you choose a 60-day elimination period, the payment for the next 30 days of disability comes to you only after you've been disabled for 30 days. So the first claim check you receive with a 60-day wait will come to you 90 days after your disability start date.

Benefit period

Benefit period refers to the duration for which you want a disability insurance paycheck — typically two years, five years, to age 65, or for your entire lifetime. Coverage to age 65 or lifetime coverage is obviously best if you can afford the cost — it costs about 30 percent more than a five-year benefit. Because many disabled people recover within five years, the five-year option is also a reasonable choice if you couldn't otherwise afford the coverage you need.

 If you have to choose the five-year plan, be prepared to make a major lifestyle change if you face a disability that continues beyond five years. The good news is that at least you'll have five years to prepare for it.

I don't recommend the two-year benefit period because a large percentage of disabilities last beyond two years.

Noncancelable versus guaranteed renewable

You have two options regarding the renewability of your coverage: *noncancelable* and *guaranteed renewable* contracts. Both promise to renew coverage to age 65. Noncancelable contracts also guarantee never to raise the price up to age 65. Guaranteed renewable contracts can raise their overall rates anytime, but they cannot single you out individually for an increase.

How important is a price guarantee? Disability insurance companies have experienced a worse-than-expected claims record over the past several years. Several companies have closed their doors, and others have merged or been sold. The number of insurance companies offering individual disability policies has decreased dramatically. Those insurers that are still active have taken some large rate increases on their guaranteed renewable contracts.

Don't let a price guarantee be the biggest issue in your selection. Buy all the coverage and features you need first. That's the highest priority. Then, if you can afford another 20 percent or so to lock in the price, do so.

Cost of living adjustment rider

If you're disabled for several years, the monthly disability check you receive has diminishing spending power. The cost of living adjustment (COLA) option annually increases your benefit while you're disabled by some predetermined percentage (usually from 3 percent to 6 percent).

If you're buying coverage to age 65, COLA is a pretty important option to include in your coverage. However, if you're buying only a five-year benefit or if you have a spouse whose projected future income will be rising dramatically, you may not need this rider.

_____

_____

_____

Future purchase option

This option guarantees, when you apply and qualify for your first policy, that, regardless of your future health, you can increase your coverage every one to three years, up to the optional limit you've purchased.

 If you think that you may need more disability coverage later, with increased expenses such as a bigger house, more children, or simple cost of living increases, I strongly recommend that you pay just a little more now for the privilege of being able to increase your benefit in the future regardless of health.

A rather high percentage of people are declined for disability insurance due to back problems, diabetes, high cholesterol, and so on. You may be such a person in the future.

The future purchase option eliminates the possibility of your being turned down for additional coverage later. And it's usually quite inexpensive. Not only does the option guarantee you the opportunity to buy additional insurance regardless of your future health, but it also greatly simplifies the purchase of such additional insurance because no applications or physical exams are required.

The difference between future purchase options and COLA options is that the purchase option increases your coverage *before* you become disabled, and COLA increases your benefits *while* you're disabled. I recommend them both.

Social insurance rider

A *social insurance rider* pays you an additional monthly benefit that is reduced or eliminated when you qualify for Social Security disability benefits or workers' compensation benefits. How this rider works varies dramatically among insurance companies. Just know that it exists and what its purpose is.

Because total disability creates such a hardship on a family, in planning I like to disregard any possible Social Security benefits — that way, they can be an inflation hedge or cushion for unplanned expenses. I recommend you do the same.

Return of premium rider

The *return of premium rider* was created for people who want their cake and want to eat it, too. After a number of years — typically 20 to 25 — the policy refunds you all your premiums, less any paid claims. Sounds great, right? It is great — except for one catch: It adds 30 percent to 40 percent a year to your costs. For that reason, and because most people may buy less insurance coverage than they need, I rarely recommend it.

Catastrophic disability rider

The *catastrophic disability* rider provides additional cash benefits over and above your loss of income to help pay the costs that come with especially disabling illnesses or injuries. Coverage triggers are usually one of the following:

- Inability to do two or more activities of daily living (like bathing, dressing, eating, and going to the bathroom) without help

- Cognitive impairments (such as head injuries or Alzheimer's disease)

- Loss of sight, hearing, speech, or two or more limbs

I strongly recommend including this optional benefit in your program unless you have a long-term-care policy, which essentially does the same thing. What makes this coverage particularly attractive is its relatively low cost.

_____

_____

_____

Own-occupation protection

Own-occupation refers to the length of time you'll be paid a full benefit when you can't perform your specific occupation but could do another. In a disability policy, the period of occupation protection is found in the policy definition for *total disability*.

The most restrictive definition is probably the one the Social Security Administration uses: complete inability to engage in *any* gainful occupation. The broadest definition is probably found in the expensive, deluxe policies offered to high-income professionals such as physicians and lawyers: the inability to perform the duties of your specific occupation.

With the Social Security definition in your policy, you may not be eligible for benefits if you can sell pencils or wash dishes. With the deluxe definition of own-occupation, if you were a radiologist making $300,000 a year with a $200,000 a year disability benefit and could no longer practice your specialty of radiology but could practice family medicine or teach radiology at the university and earn $200,000, you would still be considered totally disabled. If you're that radiologist, you could take any other job other than your job as a radiologist (for example, you could teach at the university) and get your full $200,000 benefit, plus your teacher's salary. As you might guess, this coverage is expensive. I don't think it's necessary for most people.

Most disability policies use a definition of total disability that falls somewhere between the Social Security definition and the definition found in contracts that are sold to wealthy professionals. They pay full benefits if you can't perform your particular occupation for anywhere from two to five years, sometimes ten years; then, if you're still disabled after that period, your benefits are cut off only if you can't perform another occupation for which you're reasonably suited based on your education, training, and experience. The longer the period of protection for your specific occupation, the higher the premium.

Make your decision to add an own-occupation clause based on how many years you've spent mastering your craft. A brain surgeon or a lawyer would probably want the broadest definition possible. Someone with two years of college employed as a sales representative would probably be satisfied with more limited protection on the occupation.

Always buy a disability policy that, if for whatever reason you work in another occupation that pays less than your original occupation, will still pay a proportionate/residual benefit for as long as that income difference persists. So if your original salary was $100,000 per year, and you can now only do a job that pays you, say, $50,000 per year (it decreased by 50 percent), you want disability protection that will pay you one-half of your policy benefit.

Buy Disability Insurance

You've determined how much coverage you need. You've chosen the policy features that are most important to you. You're ready to buy.

Know where to buy

If you already have a trusted insurance agent for your auto, home, or life insurance policies, she may be able to help you find the right disability insurance policy. Many — but not all — agents have disability insurance available. If your current agent does offer disability policies, make sure that she's knowledgeable about disability. If she isn't, ask for a referral to a disability insurance specialist. (For more on finding an agent, turn to Chapter 3.)

A small percentage of insurance agents deal principally with disability insurance products, and they're often quite knowledgeable about the subject. Unfortunately, they often tend to concentrate on the professional market (doctors, lawyers, CPAs, and so on). They also tend to deal in a more elite product that offers Cadillac coverage at a stiff price. Still, a disability specialist should be able to help you find a quality product at a price you can afford, or know someone who can.

Here are a few other sources to explore:

- **Your employer:** If you can get group coverage through your employer for free or at little cost, doing so is often a good idea. The major advantage of employer-based disability coverage is that you can often get the insurance even if your health is poor.

  Group coverage has some pitfalls, however. Benefits are taxable. You don't get to pick the features you want (like residual or cost of living riders). If you change jobs, you lose the insurance.

- **Association plans:** Policies from associations are often attractively priced. They usually have many of the same pitfalls as employer-paid group insurance, however, and you usually have to qualify medically. You also lose it if you drop your association membership or if the plan is discontinued.

- **Creditors:** Often sold through lending institutions, insurance from creditors is designed to pay off loans (such as payments on a car, boat, home, or credit card balance) in the event of long-term disability. Avoid this type of insurance unless you can't qualify for coverage anywhere else because of health problems. No inquiries are made as to your medical condition when you apply for some of these policies, so the rates tend to be two, three, or more times higher than preferred rates for healthy individuals. These policies also have the added disadvantage of covering only that part of your monthly living expenses that has a loan tied to it, and of expiring or running out when the loan is paid off. But if your health is poor, buy all the coverage you can get your hands on.

_____

_____

_____

Compare policies

Most agents who work with disability insurance have access to more than one company. If you've taken the time to choose an agent with plenty of expertise on disability insurance, ask her to get more than one quote. Comparing policy features and optional coverages of two or more disability policies is a challenge to the best agents and next to impossible for the consumer. So it's okay to ask her to go through the policies feature by feature so that you understand their differences.

If you have an existing or past medical issue that you or your agent are concerned might affect your chances of being approved (such as an old back injury or treatment for depression), do what I recommend to my clients: Apply simultaneously to two companies. That way you won't have to answer yes to the question on every application "Have you ever had an application for life or disability insurance declined, rated up, or otherwise modified?" That happens more often than you might think.

Don't buy based on the lowest price. Other factors to consider include the agent's expertise, the insurance company's financial strength and reputation, or special coverage features that are really important to you.

Plug Holes in Your Group Insurance Program

The good news about employer-paid group long-term disability insurance is that it's a no-cost benefit to you. The bad news is that every dime you receive is taxed as ordinary income. Plus, unlike privately owned disability insurance, group benefits are offset against anything you receive from Social Security or workers' compensation. Here are some other shortcomings of group coverage:

- **Coverage stays with the job.** You may have a right to convert the policy to an individual policy but usually with watered-down coverage and higher pricing.

- **Generally group policies don't have a cost of living adjustment, so while you're out on disability, your benefit will never increase.**

- **Many policies cover only total disabilities — no partial or residual benefits.**

_____

_____

_____

Because group benefits are taxable, the 60 percent of salary they usually pay ends up being 40 percent to 45 percent after taxes. Unless you can live comfortably on that amount, buy an individual disability policy to cover the shortfall.

A good supplement should include all the features I recommend in this chapter plus, ideally, an option to purchase additional benefits whenever you lose your group benefits for whatever reason, regardless of the condition of your health.

Take time to select a good agent who can help you identify the holes in your group plan and how to best plug them, and who is knowledgeable about supplemental policies.

_____

_____

_____

9

Buying Life Insurance

We buy life insurance because we love. We love spouses, children, and others who depend on us financially. We love them enough to acknowledge the possibility that we could die young, leaving them without our income. We love them enough to plunk down our hard-earned cash for insurance, so that if we do die early, our deaths will not burden them financially.

This chapter explains term life insurance and permanent life insurance; helps you figure out whether you need insurance and, if so, how much you need; tells you where to buy it; and dispels common myths about it.

Assess Whether You Need Life Insurance

Life insurance isn't for everyone. If no one would be hurt financially by your death, you wouldn't buy life insurance any more than you'd buy car insurance if you don't drive and don't own a car. This section gives you specific guidelines on who does and who doesn't need life insurance.

Who doesn't need life insurance

Two groups of people do *not* need life insurance:

- **Those who are financially well off enough that their survivors can meet all their financial needs and obligations using existing financial resources, without the possibility of depleting those resources:** For example, if you're married, you have one teenager, and you've managed to sock away $1 million and have paid off your house, you may not need life insurance. Your existing resources can support your child

through college and also provide your spouse with
a cushion.

- **Those whose death won't cause a hardship to others:**
  For example, if you and your spouse have no children,
  and you each earn a high enough income to support
  yourselves if the other dies, you don't need life
  insurance.

Who does need life insurance

Two groups of people *do* need life insurance:

- **Those with one or more people who depend on
  their income:** If your family depends on your income
  (whether or not your spouse works) and you don't
  have enough savings for them to live off of, your family
  will need the financial help that only life insurance
  offers. You don't have to be married or have kids to
  need life insurance, though. For example, you may be
  single but paying the bills for your elderly mother's
  assisted-living apartment — if something were to

happen to you, life insurance would make sure that she's taken care of.

- **Those who provide services that would need to be hired out in the event of their death:** If you're a stay-at-home mom, and you die while your children are young, your husband will suffer a financial loss. He'll need money to pay for childcare. He may want to hire household help as well. Over a ten-year span, childcare and occasional help around the house can cost $250,000 or more. Life insurance can make that outlay possible.

Maybe you do chores around your parents' home for them. It may cost your parents $500 per month to hire a service to do that if you die. The interest on $250,000 of life insurance can make sure those services are provided as long as your parents stay in the house. When they need more help, the money from the insurance policy can help pay nursing home costs.

Determine How Much Coverage You Need

If you die early, how much money will your loved ones need? How much will it take to pay off debt? To replace your income? Is providing funds to cover college costs for your children important, and if so, how much money will that take?

Financial experts typically recommend that you have at least enough life insurance and liquid assets to equal a multiple of five times your annual income, ignoring inflation, or seven to eight times your income factoring in inflation.

If you have children, err on the side of buying too much life insurance. I recommend that you buy enough life insurance to equal ten times your annual income, giving your surviving spouse and children a softer lifestyle with more time for each other. Why? Because life insurance is cheap — especially for young families, when the need for life insurance is greatest. When buying life insurance, aim high. For the people you love who survive you, too much is far better than too little.

What if you're insuring a stay-at-home parent who doesn't have an income? Buy enough insurance to give the surviving parent the option of paying for a nanny. Check the prices of an in-home nanny service, including cooking, cleaning, and so on, plus driving the kids where they need to go. Then multiply that cost over the number of years needed; round up for inflation.

 Buy $500,000 of life insurance — $250,000 to replace services and another $250,000 to give the surviving spouse and children a less stressful life and some extra time for each other.

Don't use retirement money to cover today's needs, even in a situation as dire as the premature death of a spouse. The survivor still needs those funds at retirement. I also don't usually recommend using home equity. It's not very liquid, and the surviving spouse will probably want to keep the house.

The Language of Life Insurance

Before looking at the different types of life insurance and the best places to buy them, here are a few definitions of insurance industry jargon:

- **Beneficiary:** The *beneficiary* is the person or organization to whom the life insurance proceeds are payable at the death of the person insured. It could be a spouse, children, a sibling, or a favorite charity. Every life insurance policy covering you — both those you buy and those at work — should name two beneficiaries: a primary beneficiary and a contingent beneficiary.

   A *primary beneficiary* is the person or organization to whom the life insurance proceeds are paid if that beneficiary is alive or in existence when you die.

   A *contingent beneficiary* is the person or organization to whom the life insurance proceeds are paid if the primary beneficiary is dead or no longer in existence. If no contingent beneficiary is named, the proceeds are paid to the estate of the primary beneficiary and possibly subject to delays and additional taxes.

- **Owner:** The *owner* of a life insurance policy may or may not be the person whose life is insured. The owner is the person or organization who controls the policy, pays the bills, chooses the beneficiary, and so on. Here are some examples of when the owner would be different from the person insured: a corporation owner insuring the life of a key scientist whose talents are vital to the company's survival; a family trust owner insuring an aging parent in order to pay estate taxes due at death; and a parent insuring the life of a child to cover final expenses.

- **Purchase options:** *Purchase options* are options available with some policies that give the person insured the right to purchase additional coverage every few years, regardless of health. Coverage is guaranteed up to a certain amount per option. The options usually cease when the person is between ages 40 and 50.

For example, a couple, both 24, are engaged to be married and are planning to buy a home and have children in two to three years. They're both in good health. They don't want to spend a lot on life insurance that they don't need right now. They would like to guarantee, while they're still healthy, that they can buy coverage later even if their health sours. They may buy starter policies for $50,000 of coverage on each and add a purchase option that every three years gives them the right to buy an additional $50,000 of coverage regardless of their health, their hobbies, or their increased size.

_____

_____

_____

- **Waiver of premium:** *Waiver of premium* is an optional coverage that suspends your life insurance premium after you've been totally disabled for (usually) six months, until you're no longer disabled. It has two disadvantages: It's more expensive than personal disability coverage, and it won't normally pay if you can work part-time. You may not need it if you have plenty of disability coverage and you've included your life insurance premium in your estimated coverage needs.

Types of Life Insurance

After you've determined how much coverage you need, you need to decide where to buy it and which type of policy is best suited to your needs. There are only two types of life insurance — permanent and term — although the two types come in many varieties. The biggest difference between them is how long the coverage lasts:

- **Permanent life insurance** covers you for your entire life. When you die, it pays the *death benefit* (the amount of money payable at the time of death).

- **Term life insurance** covers only a part of your lifetime. When that part, or *term*, ends, so does the coverage. It pays a death benefit only if you die within the designated term.

The following sections provide a brief comparison of the two types of policies. (Both types of insurance are covered in much greater detail later in this chapter.)

Permanent life insurance

Permanent life insurance is ideally suited to permanent needs. For example, you may buy permanent life insurance when you're looking to supplement retirement dollars for your surviving spouse, covering estate taxes due upon your death, or paying final expenses — burial, legal costs, and so on.

Every life insurance policy has two core parts to its price:

- **Mortality cost:** This is determined by your odds of dying at that moment. The mortality charge increases each year as you age and your risk of dying increases.

- **Policy expense cost:** This is your share of insurance company expenses (rent, staff, and agent commissions). The expense charge stays relatively constant.

Most permanent life insurance policies have level premiums for life. How is that possible if the mortality charge increases each year? The insurance company averages the increasing mortality changes over your remaining expected life. In short, you overpay in the early years so that you can underpay in the later years. That overpayment in the early years is set aside in a reserve for you, called *cash value*. If you cancel a permanent policy, by law you're entitled to get back much of those overpayments — that cash value. The cash value is minimal in the first couple of years because of heavy first-year costs — underwriting, medical exams, and agent commissions.

Permanent life insurance is considerably more expensive than term life insurance for the first several years, for the same death benefit, because permanent insurance has a cash value element.

Term life insurance

Term life insurance is ideally suited for covering life insurance needs that are not permanent. For example, you may buy term life insurance when you want to cover a 20-year mortgage, college costs for children, or family income needs while the kids are growing up.

_____

_____

_____

Term life insurance costs, unlike permanent life insurance costs, increase regularly as you age. Sometimes the increase is annual, and sometimes it's every five or ten years or more. Term insurance costs can be averaged over 10, 20, or 30 years, so the price is level for the entire term. But term insurance doesn't have a cash value element — if you drop a term insurance policy in its early years, you get no refund of any overpayment.

Because term insurance has no cash value element, premiums in the first several years are considerably lower than permanent insurance premiums for the same death benefit.

A Closer Look at Permanent Life Insurance

All permanent policies have three components: mortality costs, expense charges, and cash value. (See "Permanent life insurance," earlier in this chapter, for more information.) Insurers offering permanent insurance compete in three ways: lowering mortality costs, lowering expense charges, and having better investment yield on the cash value.

Permanent policies vary by

- Whether they guarantee mortality and expense costs
- Whether they guarantee the yield on the cash value

Three types of permanent life insurance are on the market: whole life, universal life, and variable life. Every life insurance company offers hybrids of these three. See Table 9-1 for a quick overview of how they compare.

	Whole Life	Universal Life	Variable Life
Mortality costs	Fixed	Variable	Fixed or variable
Expenses	Fixed	Variable	Fixed or variable
Cash value yield	Fixed	Variable	Variable
Investment risk to cash value	None	None	Yes
Option to vary the premium	No	Yes	Usually
Option to change the death benefit amount	No	Yes	Usually
Option to vary or suspend premiums	No	Yes	Yes

Table 9-1: *Comparing Permanent Life Insurance Types*

Whole life

People who choose whole life insurance want a lifetime policy with zero risk. They want the insurance company to guarantee, for life, the monthly cost. If an epidemic breaks out, significantly killing off a large part of the population and raising mortality costs to the insurance company, this policy cost isn't affected at all. Conversely, if science reduces heart disease rates and cures cancer, lowering deaths and mortality costs, the insurance company reaps more profits because it continues to receive the higher, guaranteed mortality charges of the whole life policy.

The same is true for expense costs. If the insurance company's expenses rise because it buys a new building or pays agents higher commissions, it can't pass on those higher costs to the whole life customers. Similarly, if it improves efficiency and cuts costs, only the insurance company reaps the benefits.

Finally, a whole life policy pays a minimal but guaranteed rate of return, usually from 2½ percent to 4 percent for life — so guaranteed, in fact, that the policy contains a page showing what the cash value will be for each year of the future. Today, 4 percent guaranteed looks good. Twenty years ago, when interest rates were in the double digits, it looked horrible.

_____

_____

_____

With whole life, the insurance company takes all the risks. You take none. The insurance company bites the bullet when things sour and reaps extra profits when things improve.

If you buy a whole life policy that offers dividends, you share a little in good years and overpay in bad years.

Universal life

In the 1980s, interest rates were rising to unexpectedly high levels, approaching 20 percent. Inflation was running rampant. Not only were the fixed rates of whole life eliminating most new sales, but existing customers were dropping their old policies in droves as, one by one, insurance companies began to offer a more flexible policy called *universal life insurance,* which has flexible rather than fixed interest rates on the cash value. At that time, a 13 percent to 14 percent return was common. Universal life later proved to be both good news and bad news for consumers.

The good news is that universal life is a flexible product. Everything that's fixed and guaranteed in a whole life policy is flexible and non-guaranteed. The risks of changes in mortality costs, expense costs, and interest rates are mostly passed on to you. If costs decrease or interest rates rise, you reap the benefit.

If costs rise or interest rates plummet, you're primarily the one who takes the hit. The only risk the insurer takes is that the universal life policy has a ceiling on how high the mortality charges can go and a guaranteed minimum interest rate on the cash value — usually 2½ percent to 4 percent.

What I like about a universal policy is its flexibility — not only its adaptability to changing market conditions, but also its flexibility with the death benefit. With whole life, if you want to raise your coverage, you have to take out an additional policy. With universal life, some companies may allow you to lower the death benefit at any time and keep the same policy. You may also be able to raise the benefit anytime, if you can prove good health, without having to buy additional policies.

I also like the ability to vary premium payments: to lower them or even temporarily suspend them, such as during hard times, or to pay in additional amounts when the rate of return is attractive — especially considering that the earnings are *tax sheltered* (free of income tax until withdrawal). With universal life, you have the option at any time of dumping large additional sums into the cash value account, subject to federal maximums.

_____

_____

_____

Be careful not to dump in additional amounts if any penalties for withdrawal exist. If there are penalties, usually it's best not to make the additional deposit.

Now the bad news. Universal life has one pitfall to be wary of, especially when interest rates are high. The sales illustration you receive estimates the amount of annual premium needing to be paid, assuming the current (high) interest rate remains constant, to fund the policy for life. When interest rates are high, that estimated premium is low because higher interest earnings will defray some of the policy costs. But when interest rates drop significantly, the original estimated premium will be inadequate to fund the costs, and you'll be required to significantly increase your contribution or cancel the policy.

If you want to be fairly safe from unexpected premium increases happening to you when you buy a universal life policy, choose a premium payment based on a very conservative interest rate. Use the minimum guaranteed rate (that is, 3 percent). If you do, you should never have to pay higher premiums later.

Variable life

When attached to life insurance, the term *variable* means that you have half a dozen or more investment options with your cash value — including investing in the stock market. The good news with variable policies is that you have the potential to outperform what you would have earned under a non-variable contract. The bad news, as with any stock market risk, is that you can lose part of your principal.

If you choose a variable policy, understand upfront that if the cash value principal declines, you'll have to make up the loss and pay increased premiums to fund the policy properly.

A Closer Look at Term Life Insurance

Term life insurance contracts are differentiated based on the length of the coverage term, whether they can be renewed, the length of the price guarantee, and whether they can be converted to permanent insurance. The following sections describe the three most common types of term life insurance.

Annual renewable term

Annual renewable term (ART) is pay-as-you-go life insurance. Each year, you pay for your mortality costs for that 12-month period, plus expenses. On each 12-month anniversary, you're a year older, your mortality costs have increased slightly, and your premium increases slightly as well.

You can renew ART policies every year simply by paying the premium. The ability to renew them could end, per the policy, in as few as ten years, but more typically it's guaranteed renewable until you're age 70 or even 100. Future prices are projected but normally not guaranteed for more than five or ten years. Premiums can increase, but most policies have guaranteed maximum prices. If your health deteriorates, your future rates won't be affected, and normally you can *convert* (that is, exchange) the policy to a permanent policy anytime, without medical questions being asked.

Fixed-rate level term

Instead of annual price increases, as with annual renewable term (see the preceding section), fixed-rate level term policies allow you to lock in pricing for anywhere from 5 to 30 years in 5-year increments. The most common options are 10, 20, and 30 years.

The process of setting up new life insurance policies (administering medical exams, ordering doctor reports, and so on) is expensive. The insurance company can spread these expenses over a longer period by selling level term insurance policies because people keep the policies longer than they keep annual term policies. As a result, insurers compete harder and offer more competitive prices for level term policies than they do for annual renewable term policies.

Most level term policies can be converted to permanent policies anytime, regardless of health (although some policies limit the conversion period to 15 years or so). Also, most can be renewed beyond the first term. Where level term policies differ most dramatically is how that renewal happens and what happens to the price.

Never buy term life insurance that doesn't have an option to convert to permanent insurance, regardless of your health. You never know what the future may hold, so keep your options open.

Fixed-rate level term policies are divided into two categories:

- **Traditionally renewable level term:** At the end of the first term, traditionally renewable level term policies renew for another period of the same length, without requiring you to requalify medically. The price changes on the renewal date, based on your age.

  Say that when you were 30 years old, you bought a ten-year traditional level term policy at preferred rates. On the renewal date ten years later, you receive a bill offering to renew for another ten years, only now at a preferred 40-year-old rate, without having to qualify medically.

- **Reentry renewable level term:** Reentry level term works like traditional level term in all respects except one: The renewal billing at the end of the original term is for your new attained age, but at sky-high rates that climb higher each year. Only if you're still healthy and can qualify medically (in other words, if you can *reenter*) can you reapply for the lowest preferred rates for another fixed term.

  Because insurance companies aren't obligated to offer the lowest rates on renewal, reentry renewable level term policies are the lowest-priced term policies in the insurance market. But their renewal price is the highest in the market if you're no longer in good health.

If you decide to buy this type of policy because of its great front-end price, give yourself a cushion. Buy it for a term of five to ten years longer than you think you'll need it to protect yourself (somewhat) from possible sky-high rates. And definitely don't use the policy for a permanent need.

Decreasing term

Decreasing term policies have coverage that reduces annually, but the premium stays level for the duration — usually 15 to 30 years. Two types of decreasing term policies exist:

- **Level decreasing term coverage** reduces coverage a flat amount each year. For example, a 25-year level decreasing term policy reduces 4 percent a year.

- **Mortgage decreasing term coverage** reduces to match a mortgage payoff. Like a mortgage, coverage reduces very slowly in the first few years and picks up steam in the later years. The rate of reduction is tied to the mortgage interest rate and the length of the mortgage.

So if you buy a 10-year, 7 percent mortgage decreasing term policy, like the mortgage balance, coverage declines much faster than a 30-year, 9 percent mortgage decreasing term policy. The 10-year, 7 percent policy is also far less expensive than the 30-year, 9 percent policy.

The good news about either type of decreasing term policy is that the rates usually won't change for the duration of the term you choose. The bad news is that your life insurance coverage is reducing at a time when your living expenses are rising. The other bad news is that your life insurance normally ends when the term ends — the policies aren't renewable. But in all likelihood, your need for life insurance hasn't ended. And the rates for this type of coverage aren't nearly as good as level reentry term rates for the same coverage period.

If you're thinking of buying a decreasing term policy, don't. Unless decreasing term life insurance coverage is court ordered (covering the mortgage of an ex-spouse and children) or mandatory as part of a loan, buy reentry level term instead of decreasing term. You get coverage that doesn't decrease and a much lower cost.

Make Your Choice

Clearly, different types of life insurance are out there. How do you choose among them? Here are a few pointers:

- **If you have a permanent need, buy permanent life insurance.** If you need it but can't afford it, buy cheap reentry level term that's convertible to permanent, regardless of your health. A permanent need is a need that, no matter how old you are today, will require cash for your survivors when you die — paying estate taxes or providing supplemental income to a surviving spouse.

- **If you have a nonpermanent need, buy term life insurance.** Examples of nonpermanent needs include covering living expenses while the children are growing up or paying for the children's college education.

- **Buy annual renewal term insurance if your need is pressing for only a year or two, but only if the price is less than that of a ten-year reentry level term policy.**

- **Buy reentry level term if your need is great and your budget is small, such as if you're a parent with young children.** However, make sure that you're clear on when the initial level term period ends. If you still need life insurance at that time, you may need to convert what you have into a much higher-priced permanent policy if you can't qualify medically for reentry. For that reason, I recommend that you buy reentry term insurance for a period of at least five to ten years longer than you think you need it. Also, because you want the company to be around when you convert, make sure that the quality of the insurance company is high. I suggest an A.M. Best rating of A or better. (See Chapter 3 for details.)

For a small charge, some reentry term products offer a guarantee that, at the end of the first level term period, you can renew for another term at the low reentry rate regardless of your health. Unless you're 100 percent sure that you won't need coverage beyond the first term, buy this option if it's available.

- **Buy only guaranteed renewable and convertible term products.** You never know what the future may hold.
- **Buy traditional non-reentry level term coverage anytime you find its pricing reasonably close to reentry term costs, or if you're willing to pay extra**

for the peace of mind of keeping preferred rates for another term without ever having to requalify.

- **Unless the price is significantly lower, always buy privately owned term life insurance rather than the optional group life insurance through employers, associations, or creditors and banks.** Coverage from the latter sources can end (such as coverage from your employer ending when you leave your job).

- **Be very wary about buying decreasing term life insurance.** Prices usually aren't that competitive, and coverage is normally not renewable. Plus, people's coverage needs rarely decrease.

Life Insurance Sources

After you've determined how much coverage you need and the type of policy — term or permanent — that best suits your needs, you can search out the best place to buy what you need.

Buying with an agent

Permanent insurance is available almost exclusively from insurance agents. I recommend that you buy permanent insurance only from a top agent. Keep in mind that permanent insurance, due to its complexity and cash value element, requires added expertise in choosing among different products.

Buying term insurance is a completely different issue. Unlike almost any other kind of insurance, term insurance is close to a commodity. Term policies are the least complex policies you can buy. The policy boils down to one sentence: "If you die, we pay." Because — unlike most other policies — there aren't a lot of hidden exclusions, limitations, and other dangers, buying it direct, without an agent, is less risky than buying any other policy direct.

Still, using an agent doesn't cost that much more (if anything). I recommend using one, but pick only a skilled agent. Hiring the best won't cost you a dime more, because all agents get paid about the same amount, determined by the premium you pay. (See Chapter 3 for tips on choosing an expert.)

A good agent can help you determine the right amount of coverage, determine the best type of term insurance product to use, set up the policy owner and beneficiary properly, and be an advocate for you if you're having problems with the insurance company. A top agent can also help you choose a financially solid company that will endure. And finally, if your application is rejected due to health, weight, or other problems, a good agent can help you search for a company that will insure you.

Life insurance is available from career life insurance agents whose primary occupation is the sale of life insurance, from the agent who helps you with your auto and homeowner's insurance, and from many financial planners.

Career life insurance agents

The principal advantage of career life insurance agents is that life insurance is their specialty. They tend to have a higher level of expertise, especially if they have more than five years in the business. Life insurance agents who have taken advanced classes and earned professional designations, such as the Certified Life Underwriter (CLU), are especially good bets.

Be careful of inexperienced agents, especially if you have complex needs. Many don't last. The washout rate for life insurance agents is one of the highest of any profession — close to 90 percent in the first two years. As you can guess, most new agents also have less expertise than experienced agents. (In many states, a person can legally sell life insurance with just a week of schooling.)

If you work with a new agent and you have any concerns about what's being recommended to you, get a second opinion. If you decide to work with an agent, you may get a lot of pressure to buy permanent life insurance when you're asking for term life insurance. The dramatically higher commission that agents earn by selling permanent insurance compared to term insurance may be the reason. If the agent who's "helping" you insists that permanent insurance is your best option when your need isn't permanent, walking away from that agent may be your only option. Of course, some real pros, who care about your welfare, may also believe that permanent insurance is the only way to go. After all, permanent insurance is always going to be there for you and your loved ones, as long as you pay the premiums.

Multiple policy agents

Many agents who sell auto and home insurance also have life insurance licenses. But less than half know much about life insurance or even actively sell it. And probably only 20 percent are quite knowledgeable about the subject.

If you like your current auto and homeowner's agent's skills in those areas, but he isn't an expert on life insurance, ask for a referral to a life insurance specialist. If your agent is good at his specialty, chances are excellent that the agent he refers you to will also be good.

If your current agent is skilled with life insurance, working with him in that area, too, is to your advantage. Having one agent for everything simplifies your life. And the washout rate on these multiple policy agents is very small.

Financial planners

Two types of people licensed to sell life insurance fit the broad *financial planner* category:

- Money managers who primarily dispense investment advice but also are licensed to sell life insurance
- Career life agents who also offer investments

_____

_____

_____

The primary difference between the two is that the former more often recommend buying term life insurance with your investments separate, whereas the latter often recommend permanent life insurance with its cash value as a part of your investment portfolio.

 If you're considering buying life insurance from a financial planner, a pretty safe bet is that those who recommend term insurance for your nonpermanent needs are the better choice. Permanent insurance is not considered a good investment product.

Buy permanent insurance if it's the best insurance for your needs, but don't buy it solely as an investment, for three reasons:

- **Permanent life is not portable.** If something better comes along, it's hard to move without penalty.

- **The mortality charges are usually higher than those for term insurance.** To get a true reflection of the rate of return on the cash value of a permanent policy, you need to deduct the hidden costs of those extra mortality and expense charges. How? By shopping for the lowest term life policy, requesting that the agent disclose those same charges in the permanent policy, and then subtracting the difference between the two results from the cash value gain.

- **Permanent life insurance has a heavy front-end cost due to the high sales commission, which significantly affects the cash value performances.**

Buying without an agent

If you're considering buying term life insurance direct from a toll-free number or on the job, first check with your favorite agent to see whether she can match the price. She probably can — in which case, use an agent. If your agent can't match the quote or come close, consider paying the agent a fee (perhaps $200) to review your plans and make sure that you're not shooting yourself in the foot.

The following sources of term life insurance allow you to buy without an agent:

- **The Internet:** Several sites are set up to comparison-shop term life insurance, but I don't recommend buying any insurance this way unless you yourself are an expert. (See Chapter 3 on buying insurance right.)

- **Creditors:** Banks, mortgage companies, and credit card companies regularly solicit their customers to buy *credit life insurance* from them to pay off any balance if the customer dies. Look at what they get: If you buy the insurance from your mortgage company, for example, it makes a nice upfront commission on the sale, and later, if you die, it gets paid your outstanding balance. What a good deal (for them).

  But how good is the deal for you? Not very. Life insurance rates from creditors are usually much higher than on the open market. And the creditor — not your survivors — is the beneficiary. Unless your health makes you uninsurable through traditional life insurance sources, avoid buying insurance from your creditors.

- **Associations:** Many groups and associations offer term life insurance as a membership benefit. Sometimes the price is fantastic. Most of the time, the price is mediocre. The problem is that if you leave the association or the association quits offering the coverage, you lose your life insurance.

_____

_____

_____

As a general rule, don't buy life insurance from an association. However, do buy as much as you can if you're uninsurable and the insurer asks no medical questions.

- **Group life:** Take all the free life insurance your employer offers you. If and only if your health is poor and you can't qualify for other types of life insurance, buy all the supplemental life insurance your employer offers on a nonmedical basis. (Sometimes that can be $50,000 or more.) If you're healthy, don't buy any more than the free coverage paid for by your employer through work. Buy it privately. Why? Two reasons: You lose group insurance when you leave the job, and the rates are almost always higher than on the open market if you're in good health.

- **Direct mail and telemarketing phone solicitations:** Again, unless they offer guaranteed coverage and you're otherwise uninsurable, stay away from direct mail and toll-free number sources. Most have a fly-by-night feel. Plus, they rarely offer prices that can compete with those you can get in the market if you're healthy.

Common Life Insurance Mistakes

People make all kinds of mistakes when they buy life insurance. This section fills you in on the most common ones so that you can avoid falling into any traps.

Trading cash value for death protection needs

Being under-insured with permanent life insurance may be the biggest single mistake that people make in buying life insurance. They get swayed by the lure of the investment portion or cash value of the policy but can't afford to have their cake and eat it, too. In other words, they can't afford to pay for all the death protection they need plus the investment, so they buy a cash value policy with less death protection than they need in order to have some investment — something to show for it in the end when they don't (unlike the rest of us) die. However, when they do die, their family doesn't have enough money to live on, creating a serious financial problem.

_____

_____

_____

The most important thing about life insurance is the protection it offers. So determine how much life insurance you need by using a credible method. Then buy as much of that protection as you can afford, using term insurance, even lower-cost reentry products if necessary. If your budget has something left over, only then is it okay to look at permanent life products for part of your coverage. Never trade critical protection for less-important investment opportunities.

Buying your life insurance in pieces

Buying life insurance in pieces is a lot more expensive than covering all your needs in one policy. Plus, buying in pieces leaves you vulnerable to a gap in your coverage. Examples of piecemeal buying are having mortgage insurance through your lending institution, credit card insurance through your credit card company, supplemental group life insurance at work, and so on. With some of these insurances, you don't have to qualify medically; therefore, if you're in poor health or near death, buy all you can. Otherwise, they're often three or four times the price of what you would pay if you're in good health.

When buying life insurance, figure out how much insurance you need to do the whole job and buy *one* policy. It's smarter and cheaper. Plus you have the advantage of a trusted professional agent to help with determining how much coverage you need, the type of policy, and so on.

Buying accidental death/travel accident coverage

Both accidental death and travel accident policies are varieties of Las Vegas insurance, transferring only the accidental portion of your risk. In other words, you have no coverage for death from natural causes. Buying these policies is an especially bad move if you buy them in lieu of the full life insurance you really need. My belief about travel accident coverage is that anyone who buys it at the airport or from a travel agent is really saying, "I'm not comfortable with the amount of life insurance I have." If you need insurance to cover a flight you're taking, you also need it for driving down the street, potential heart attacks, and the like.

When buying life insurance, buy only coverage that pays for any death — natural or accidental.

Covering the children in lieu of the parents

When your child is born, you try to be a responsible parent. You're deluged with a lot of solicitations about life insurance. You have hopes and dreams for your children, so you buy a nice cash value policy on your baby. It's understandable — you're so proud. But the economic effect on the family of a child's death is minimal compared to the major impact that one of the baby's parents dying would have.

When a child is born, seriously reevaluate and raise the amount of life insurance coverage that you and your spouse have.

Being unrealistic about how much you can afford to pay for life insurance

I can't tell you how many times I've seen young people commit more money than they can actually afford to a large cash value life insurance policy and then two or three years later have to drop it and take a large financial loss — and perhaps even be exposed to the risk of a death without insurance. I recommend term insurance for young families. It provides the most coverage for the money spent. If you want a permanent policy later with more bells and whistles, you can always convert your term policy.

10

Changing Your Insurance When Your Life Changes

When you experience a major life change, you need to change your insurance coverage. The insurance plan you had before the change often won't cover some of the new risks you've taken on during and after the change. This chapter shows you how to manage the insurance risks of life's more common changes — from the cradle to the grave.

Getting Married

From getting engaged up to the wedding ceremony, you face special risks. This section has strategies to help you manage them.

Getting engaged

If a valuable ring is involved in the engagement and you want it insured in case it's lost or stolen, you should schedule it as an addendum to a homeowner's or renter's policy. A basic homeowner's policy provides little or no jewelry coverage, especially for the loss of a diamond or other gem, so the ring must be scheduled. If you already have the wedding rings and if they have any value, you may want to schedule them as well.

Generally, the ring should be insured under the policy of its owner. If the owner still lives with her parents, add the ring to her parents' homeowner's policy. If the owner rents but has no renter's policy, it's time to get one (see Chapter 5).

Living together before marriage

Set up a homeowner's or renter's policy in *both* names. If you buy the insurance under only your name, your partner has no personal liability coverage under your policy for activities — such as injuring someone while playing racquetball. Plus, your partner's personal belongings won't be covered. Both of your names need to be on the policy in order for both of you to be protected.

_____

_____

_____

Move both your car insurance policies to the same insurance company and buy the same liability limits on each policy. Your personal auto policy won't cover you while you're driving your partner's car. (It excludes coverage on cars you have regular access to.) Being insured with the same company assures you that your policy terms will be identical, no matter which car you drive — which will also make for a far easier claim experience. Buying the same liability limits assures that the same amount of money will be available to each of you for lawsuits regardless of which car you're driving. If you buy $300,000 of coverage and your partner has $50,000 of coverage, when you drive your partner's car the only coverage you have is his $50,000. The only way you can get $300,000 of coverage, when you live together, is for him to have the same $300,000 liability coverage as you have. If your partner won't agree to the same coverage, don't *ever* drive his car.

Some auto insurance companies offer an optional coverage called *extended non-owned liability coverage*, which extends your coverage to his vehicle, and vice versa. If your insurer offers it, add it to both policies. It's not expensive.

Tying the knot

After you get married, set up homeowner's or renter's insurance in both names (see Chapter 5). Make sure the property limit is high enough to cover your belongings as well as your wedding gifts. Also, combine your vehicles on one car insurance policy (see Chapter 4 on buying car insurance and Chapter 5 on buying homeowner's or renter's insurance.).

If you're both working, continue your group health coverage if it's provided to you by your employers. If one of you doesn't have health coverage through work, add the uninsured spouse to the insured spouse's group policy. You generally have 30 days from the wedding date to do so without having to *qualify medically* (prove that you're in good health). After 30 days, you can be declined due to poor health.

Make sure you have enough life insurance to pay for a funeral and other final expenses. Most jobs include enough free life insurance to cover these costs. If one of you has life insurance through work and the other doesn't, add the uninsured spouse to the insured spouse's group policy. You can also buy an individual policy. (Chapter 9 has tips on estimating life insurance needs.) Be sure to change the beneficiaries on all life insurance policies — individual or group — to each other.

Don't overlook long-term disability insurance, especially if you need two incomes to make ends meet (see Chapter 8).

Be careful of contracts you're asked to sign related to the wedding reception. Make sure the terms are reasonable. I had one client show me a restaurant rental contract where the wedding party had to agree to be responsible not only for injuries they caused but also for injuries the restaurant caused, like food poisoning. Sign something like that, and you'll be in deep trouble — with the possibility of no insurance — if a guest is injured at the reception! Have an attorney review contracts like this, before you sign them, where there are substantial risks. You're better off changing the location of the reception than paying thousands of dollars to defend and pay judgments against the restaurant for its negligence. Check with your agent to make sure that your personal liability coverage — home and/or umbrella — will protect you if you do get sued for injuries or property damage at the reception.

_____

_____

_____

Building or Remodeling a Home

Whether you're building your dream home or remodeling your current one, you've taken on a lot of additional risks, many of which are not automatically insured. Enjoy the excitement, but make sure that your insurance is adequate for the new risks in your life. Here's a list of some of those risks and how to handle them:

- **Property damage to new construction from fire, wind, vandalism, and so on:** If you're building a new home, have a clear understanding with the builder, in writing, as to who is responsible for the property insurance. Require that the party who buys the insurance also names the other party as loss payee. Require that proof of the insurance be provided prior to the start of construction. If you, as the homeowner, are responsible for the insurance, buy a homeowner's policy rather than a builder's risk policy.

Homeowner's coverage is much more comprehensive and includes, at no extra charge, liability coverage for job-site injuries.

If you're remodeling, increase your homeowner's building-coverage limit, at the time the work starts, to the revised cost to replace your home with the improvements.

- **Theft of building materials:** Normally materials aren't covered until they're installed in your home. Either contractually require the contractor to be responsible for all materials until they're installed, or add a theft of building materials endorsement to your homeowner's policy and delete the endorsement when everything is installed.

- **Lawsuits from job-site injuries:** These are usually covered by your homeowner's policy, but this is a good time to reevaluate your personal liability limits. Consider adding an umbrella policy if you don't already have one (see Chapter 6). Also, in your construction contract, require the contractor to defend you and pay any judgment against you for injuries or property damage he or his crew cause. Request proof of the contractor's general liability insurance before work starts. If he doesn't have insurance, you're much more apt to be sued yourself if someone gets hurt.

- **Workers' compensation claims filed against you for medical bills and lost wages from any worker injured on the job:** This risk is *not* covered by your homeowner's policy. Require written proof from your contractor that he has workers' compensation insurance covering all workers before any work starts. Run all labor costs — even if you're paying your friends to chip in — through the contractor, so that you're not at risk for anyone's injuries.

  Another option is to buy your own workers' compensation policy for the period of construction, especially if you're acting as your own general contractor. Don't start new construction without someone — you or the contractor — having workers' compensation insurance in place.

- **Injuries and property damage that happen to you or your home after the work is completed:** For example, the furnace blows soot through the house, a defective fireplace causes a major building fire, or the roof leaks from a defective installation. Require in your construction contract that the contractor provide you proof of general liability insurance, including completed operations coverage, which covers this kind of claim. If there are injuries or damages later, you may have a source of insurance to collect from.

- **The contractor skipping out and not paying subcontractors, who then file liens against your property:** Require the contractor to get lien waivers signed by all subcontractors prior to your paying for the work. Or, if he's not agreeable to that, pay the subcontractors directly.

- **Misunderstandings between you and the contractor, causing significant frustration and financial loss:** Always work with a contract and a good attorney. Incorporate into the contract the issues addressed in this list.

_____

_____

_____

Becoming a New Parent

When you're expecting the birth of your first child, it's time to revisit three types of insurance that may need to be changed:

- **Health insurance:** Under many health plans, newborns cease to be covered 30 days after birth unless you notify your health insurance company within that 30-day period requesting that your child be added to your coverage, so call the insurance company immediately — don't wait 30 days. If you're married, you may have a choice between the mother's policy and the father's policy. If you do, compare costs, features, and the freedom to choose doctors.

- **Life insurance:** When a child is born, you have to buy or significantly raise your *own* life insurance protection to make sure that the baby will be protected if you die. Don't forget to insure the stay-at-home parent if one of you will be staying home. This is also a good time to reassess life insurance beneficiaries and change your contingent beneficiary to "all surviving children" instead of "my brother Ralph." (See Chapter 9 on how to determine life insurance needs.)

- **Disability insurance:** If you've put off buying this coverage, now is a good time to rethink your decision. The loss of a paycheck would be a bigger hardship now that you have a new baby. (See Chapter 8 for more on disability insurance.)

Hiring a Nanny

You've recently become proud parents. As soon as you found out you were expecting, you probably started considering your childcare options. Do you put the baby in daycare, or do you hire a nanny to care for your child in your home?

If you go the nanny route, you have a couple of options. You can hire a nanny through a professional nanny service, which costs quite a bit more but has a number of advantages:

- The agency screens candidates and checks references for you.
- The agency provides temporary nannies to fill in when your nanny is ill, takes a vacation, or simply doesn't show up.

- The agency carries liability insurance in case one of your children is injured in the nanny's care. (Most self-employed nannies don't have any liability insurance.)

- The agency carries workers' compensation insurance covering the nanny if she's injured on the job, regardless of fault. This significantly reduces the chance of the nanny suing you for a job-related injury.

- The agency does all the withholding, pays all the payroll taxes, and issues the paychecks to the nanny so you don't have to.

Not all nanny services provide all these benefits, so make sure you understand what you're getting into before you sign on the dotted line.

A second option is to hire your own nanny. You can hire her as an independent contractor, a common approach but one that has liability and potential tax consequences that aren't, in my opinion, worth taking. A better, safer choice is to hire your nanny as an employee. You'll need to cut her a paycheck and do some withholding. Depending on what state you're in, you may need to buy workers' compensation insurance for her. (Check with your state's department of labor for information on workers' compensation requirements for domestic employees.

Many states exempt you from having to provide the coverage for a single employee.) If you're required to buy workers' compensation insurance, you benefit in two ways:

- The nanny is prohibited by law from suing you if she gets hurt on the job.

- The nanny can collect for her medical bills and lost wages from your workers' compensation policy, regardless of how it happened.

For more information on household employees and the IRS rules, go to www.irs.gov/publications/p926/index.html or call 800-829-3676 and request Publication 926: Household Employer's Tax Guide.

If your nanny will be driving your child or picking up your child as part of her duties, your child could be injured in a car accident caused by the nanny's negligence. Here are some steps to take to protect yourself and your child before you hire the nanny:

- **Get her signed permission to check her driving record.** Request her driver's license number and vehicle plate number. Then provide both numbers and her signed permission to your auto insurance agent and request her driving and accident records. If her record isn't clear for at least three years, look into other candidates.

- **Get proof of her automobile insurance liability coverage if she uses her own car.** Make sure both her liability coverage and uninsured/under-insured motorists coverage are at least $300,000. If not, ask her to increase them to at least that level. Offer to pay the additional cost if need be. The cost for extra liability coverage is small — $50 to $100 a year tops.

- **Add her as an occasional operator to your car insurance if she'll be using your car regularly.**

For more information on hiring a nanny, go to www.nannyjobs.com/ResourceEmployers.aspx.

Moving to a New Place

Moving is nearly always a huge undertaking, full of heavy lifting, hard work, and a year's worth of stress. The last thing you want to think about when you're planning a move is insurance, but if you overlook insurance, your move may be even more stressful than it already is. When you move, your belongings may be in storage or in transit for some period of time. If your new home is ready for move-in right away, your belongings will, at the very least, be in transit on the moving truck for however long it takes to get from your old home to your new one. And if your new home isn't ready yet, your stuff may be in storage for days, weeks, or even months. If your things are in storage, you may have to live in a motel with some of your belongings.

To cover your personal property that's in transit and/or in storage, don't cancel the homeowner's or renter's policy insuring your old home. Then, manage your risks as follows:

- **Property being moved while in transit:** Basic homeowner's insurance covers only specific losses like collision and theft. It won't cover all losses, such as breakage of furniture and electronics from load shifting. So add special perils contents coverage to your homeowner's policy, insuring the contents in the home you're leaving. This form covers almost any loss outside of a few exclusions such as breakage of fragile items (dishes and the like). If you want fragile items covered for breakage, you'll need to schedule them. (Or pay the movers to do the packing and buy breakage coverage from them.)

- **Property in storage:** Basic homeowner's policies do cover, in full, all personal property in a locked storage facility up to the contents policy limit. But the types of losses covered are limited to fire, wind, vandalism, theft, and so on. No coverage exists, for example, for water damage from roof leaks or groundwater damage of any kind. To cover yourself, add special perils contents coverage, which covers almost all losses, including water damage from roof leaks. Although it excludes groundwater damage at home, it covers groundwater damage *away* from home, such as for items in storage.

- **Property at your temporary location:** Your homeowner's policy covers any property you have with you in a temporary location up to the contents policy limit for up to 30 days. Beyond 30 days, coverage drops to 10 percent of the policy limit on contents. If you're going to be in that location longer than 30 days, you don't need to make special insurance arrangements to cover your stuff if you're okay with the 10 percent limit. If you're not, ask your agent to negotiate an extension for the time you need. If that fails, buy renter's insurance. (If you're storing most of your stuff, the 10 percent limit is usually plenty for what you have with you.)

- **Damage to the moving truck, if you decide to move yourself:** In the rental contract you sign, you're liable for anything — even storm damage. Coverage is available from the rental agency, but it's expensive. Decline coverage from the rental agency if you have both collision and comprehensive coverage on at least one of your cars. The coverage you have on your own car will transfer to the truck. If you don't have the coverage, either have your agent add the coverages to your car insurance policy or buy the coverage from the rental agency.

  Many car insurance policies limit this coverage to trucks with a gross vehicle weight rating not exceeding 10,000 pounds. Ask the rental agency how much the truck weighs, and if it exceeds 10,000 pounds, call your agent to see whether your policy has that 10,000-pound limitation. If it does, buy the coverage from the rental agency.

- **Liability when operating the rental truck for injuries and property damage to the public:** As long as you have personal auto insurance, no additional coverage is necessary. Personal auto insurance fully covers this risk up to your policy limit. (It may be a good time, though, to reevaluate your auto liability limits. Should they be increased? Or is it time to buy a personal umbrella policy?) If you don't have personal auto insurance, you can usually get the liability insurance from the rental agency where you'll also have to get your collision damage coverage.

When you're between homes and have temporary living and storage arrangements, you need personal property and liability coverage at multiple locations. Don't cancel the homeowner's or renter's policy on the property you're moving from until coverage at the new, permanent location begins. That way, the contents and liability coverage from the homeowner's or renter's policy will continue to cover your needs while you're in transition.

A fairly common twist to the previous moving example occurs when, instead of doing all the moving yourself, you hire a moving and storage company to move your stuff to their warehouse, store it for you, and then move it again to the new home. Aren't the movers liable for anything that happens, including breakage, damage, and even water damage in storage?

_____

_____

_____

It depends. If you don't make special arrangements, the fine print in your moving contract limits the moving company's liability for damage to your stuff to a fraction of its value, typically 50 cents per pound! (For your $2,000 big-screen TV that weighs 80 pounds, they would owe you only 80 multiplied by 0.5, or $40.) The contract usually also exempts the movers from damage they didn't cause, such as flood damage to the property in storage.

Moving contracts are usually very anti-consumer. Read them carefully, or have your insurance agent read them, so you know what you're responsible for before a claim happens. The moving company may insure the full value of your property if you pay them a little extra, but still not for every kind of loss. Many still exclude acts of God or groundwater, and they usually won't cover breakage unless you pay them to do the packing.

Before buying the optional insurance from the moving company, send a copy of the coverage to your agent or attorney to make sure that there aren't any nasty surprises. I still prefer adding the special perils contents endorsement to your homeowner's or renter's policy, if you don't already have it. It's less expensive than the moving company's insurance and usually is far better coverage, except for the fact that it excludes breakage of dishes and the like. If you want these items covered, get the mover's insurance.

Sending a Child to College

When you're getting ready to send your kid to college, your insurance needs may change. Here's a quick list of the types of insurance you'll want to look at and potentially alter:

- **Health insurance:** Most colleges offer optional student health coverage — buy it if it's inexpensive. This coverage enables your college student to access care at the student health center. (The more convenient the care is, the more likely he'll be to get the care he needs right away.) Don't rely on student health insurance exclusively, though — it's usually not that strong. Continue major medical coverage on your child as well, for the big stuff.

- **Car insurance:** Most insurance companies give a 10 percent to 25 percent discount for a B average or better, and another 30 percent to 40 percent (or more) discount if the student attends college over 100 miles from home and has no car at school. Ask for the good student and distant student discounts.

- **Personal property:** Most homeowner's policies extend your homeowner's contents coverage to your child's belongings at school. Most policies stop coverage after 45 days without occupancy (meaning your kid can't leave the stuff unattended for the summer and still have it covered by insurance, but he can leave it over winter break). If he isn't spending the summer at school, bring the stuff home or store it.

   Your kid's expensive valuables or expensive laptop computer can be scheduled on your homeowner's policy for the best possible insurance — covering everything from breakage to soda spilled on the keyboard.

- **Your liability for your kid's apartment:** Many college students, especially after a year or two, opt for an apartment off-campus rather than a dorm. Do not cosign a lease to help your kid qualify for the apartment. Sign a rent guarantee instead, which guarantees that you'll make the rent payment if your student doesn't. Being a cosigner makes you potentially suable for everything that goes on in that apartment (like serious injuries at college parties).

If you've already made the mistake of cosigning the lease for your college student's apartment, buy some liability coverage for yourself. Adding the apartment to your homeowner's and umbrella liability policies should only cost about $20 a year.

Divorcing

Ending a marriage is tough enough without the additional stress of insurance disputes. Here's some advice to help you minimize problems.

Before the divorce

Because the divorce process takes a long time, spouses often live separately while still being legally married. Before your divorce is finalized, address a couple of insurance issues:

- **As soon as you both agree to start divorce proceedings, separate your cars onto separate policies.** Still list both names if the vehicle titles are in both names, but your name should be first on your own policy; use your address on your own policy, too, so that the bills are mailed to you. This strategy gives you the best possible coverage and it keeps you from being victimized if your soon-to-be ex (intentionally or unintentionally) fails to pay the premium.

- **Cover yourself and your property if you move out of the house.** If you rented a new place, the primary homeowner's policy on the house you shared with your soon-to-be-ex provides no theft coverage and no liability coverage at your new apartment.

  At the very least, get liability coverage for injuries and property damage at the apartment. The least expensive way to do that is through a policy endorsement added to the primary homeowner's policy (and umbrella policy if you have one), at a cost of about $20 a year.

If theft is a concern, buy a renter's policy covering the apartment — in both your name and your spouse's name until the divorce is final. Costs for these policies start at $150 a year and up.

In a separation and pending the divorce, don't remove the person who moved out of the house from the homeowner's insurance, even if the insurance company requests it. Both parties must remain as co-named insureds on the face sheet of the policy. Until the divorce is final, both parties still equally own the home, both have an interest in the house if it is damaged or destroyed, and both need worldwide personal liability coverage.

After the divorce

If you haven't already split up the car insurance, do so now. Do not remove either spouse from the homeowner's policy until the deed has been changed.

Be careful: Many times, following a divorce, the home is put up for sale and both parties continue to own it until it's sold. If that's the case, don't remove either party's name from the policy until the sale is finalized.

_____

_____

_____

If either spouse has been covered under the other's group health insurance policy, that spouse will lose health insurance coverage when the divorce is final. If you're the one losing coverage, here are my suggestions:

- **If you have group coverage available on your job, request coverage from your employer right away, to start the date your coverage ends under your ex's policy.** If you do so within 30 days of the divorce, you're usually guaranteed coverage without having to qualify medically.

- **If you don't have coverage available through your job, exercise your COBRA right to continue coverage under your ex's group policy (if you're eligible) while applying for your own individual health policy.** See Chapter 7 for more information on COBRA and HIPAA rights.

Make sure that you're the owner of your life insurance policy. Have the billing address changed to your address. And change the beneficiaries from your ex to your children or another person. Reevaluate your life insurance needs. You may need less or, if you're a single parent, you may need substantially more. (See Chapter 9 for tips on estimating your life insurance needs.)

If you declined disability insurance coverage in the past because your spouse's income more than covered the bills, buy it now. If your paycheck stops because of a disability, you'll be hurting if you don't have this vital coverage. (See Chapter 8 for tips on buying long-term-disability insurance.)

Retiring

When you're retiring, you need to address some specific and unique insurance issues. To start, change the use of your car to pleasure use — you'll save about 15 percent to 20 percent on your car insurance. Also, make sure you're getting any senior discounts the insurance company offers.

Take the approved defensive driver course if your insurance company gives you enough credit off your premium. In Minnesota, for example, seniors get a 10 percent credit off their rates for three years. Every state is different, so check with your agent.

What to do about your health insurance depends on your age and whether you qualify under the federal COBRA law (turn to Chapter 7 for more on COBRA continuation rights):

- **If you (or your spouse) are less than 62 years old or if you're not eligible for COBRA,** apply for guaranteed individual coverage under federal HIPAA laws for you and/or your spouse, and keep it until you're both 65 years old and qualify for Medicare. If you're healthy enough to qualify for an individual plan in the open market, and if the rates and/or coverage are better than your HIPAA plan, go that route instead.

- **If you're between 62 and 65 years old and you do qualify for COBRA,** continue your health insurance through your previous employer for up to 36 months, or until you qualify for Medicare. If you're healthy enough to qualify for an individual plan that is less expensive or offers better coverage than your COBRA plan, apply for that plan and, if approved, keep the individual plan to age 65 and drop the COBRA coverage.

- **If you're 65 or older,** apply for both Part A and Part B of Medicare directly from Medicare. Once approved, apply for a good Medicare supplement policy to plug the shortcomings of Medicare. Also apply for Part D (prescription drug coverage).

If you apply for a Medicare supplement policy and Part D within six months of turning 65 or losing your group coverage, whichever is later, there are no health questions — coverage is guaranteed. (See Chapter 7 for more on your COBRA and HIPAA rights.)

Also, reassess your needs relative to life insurance. With less income, you may need less life insurance. If you still need life insurance and your health is poor, consider converting the group life insurance you had at work to a permanent, personally owned policy. Most group life insurance policies give you that option if you apply within 30 days of retirement.

Transferring Property to Trusts

Attorneys are increasingly recommending to their older clients that they transfer ownership of their home (and sometimes personal property such as cars and boats) to a trust or to their adult children — usually for tax reasons. Although these transfers may save on taxes, they result in some serious insurance gaps if changes aren't made to the insurance program of the old and the new owner.

For example, Betty, age 68, follows her attorney's advice and transfers ownership of her $400,000 home and all its contents to a trust, with a provision that gives Betty the right to continue to live in the house for as long as she wants. If Betty has a $400,000 homeowner's policy on the house and a tornado destroys it, how much will the policy pay Betty? Not much. She's no longer the owner. And the trust has lost a $400,000 asset because the trust had no insurance on the home. Betty's policy wouldn't pay the trust because the trust isn't named on the policy.

If you transfer ownership of your home to anyone else, you no longer can collect under your policy as the owner. The new owners cannot collect under your policy either. You must make some changes to your homeowner's insurance at the moment ownership is transferred, covering the new owner's ownership interest.

The former owner of the property should co-name the new owner — the trust or the adult children — as co-named insureds on the declarations page (the coverage summary page) of the policy. This way, the old and new owners are equally protected against damage if they're both named and, as a bonus, the old and new owners are also equally protected for lawsuits. List any trust as a co-named insured on the umbrella liability policy as well.

If adult children, rather than a trust, receive the property, I recommend, in addition to being a co-named insured on the parent's policy, that the adult children extend their home and umbrella liability policies to the new location. This extension should cost about $20 a year.

Coping with a Loved One's Death, and Caring for Your Loved Ones after You're Gone

One of the greatest acts of love is buying more life insurance than your survivors will need. Make sure they know about it, as well as where you keep the policies. If they can't be found, they'll never be collected on. Even if they eventually are found, searching for them is an unnecessary and traumatic experience for the survivors.

Make a list of every life insurance policy you have, make several copies of the list, and give the copies to two or more people. Include on the list the following:

- The insurance company name and address
- The policy number
- The effective date
- The death benefit amount
- The beneficiary
- The agent's name and phone number
- The location of the original policies

Here's a checklist for the survivors:

- Gather the original life policies (or the inventory form, if you have one). Ask the insurance companies to mail you their claim forms. Have certified copies of the death certificate and copies of the newspaper obituary to file with each claim form.
- Don't take the deceased off any insurance policy, including the personal umbrella policy, until the deceased's

ownership interests have been properly transferred. Otherwise, the estate is exposed, with no insurance.

- If a vehicle is involved, notify the auto insurance company of any new drivers. If the deceased is not married, add the executor as a co-named insured onto the deceased's auto policy until the estate is settled. Otherwise, the car (for most uses) will be uninsured.

- If you've been covered as a family member under the deceased's group health insurance policy, you may have the right to continue coverage for up to 36 months under COBRA. You're also guaranteed the right, under federal HIPAA law, to apply for and receive an individual policy. If you're in good health, apply for an individual health policy.

- If the deceased had disability insurance, cancel it. There may be a refund due you on prepaid premiums.

About the Author

Jack Hungelmann's policy knowledge, problem-solving expertise, and coverage analysis skills were gained through more than 2,000 hours of education and 35 years in the insurance business as a claims adjuster, agent, and consultant. He has advised individuals and commercial enterprises on their insurance needs and has earned several distinguished designations. Among these are the Certified Insurance Counselor (CIC), the Chartered Property and Casualty Underwriter (CPCU), and the Associate in Reinsurance (ARe).

Jack graduated from the University of Minnesota in 1969 and has taught professional continuing education classes for the CPCU Society and the National Alliance for Insurance Education & Research. He has been published numerous times in *American Agent & Broker* magazine. He has written and continues to write quarterly articles on personal risk management and insurance for the website of the International Risk Management Institute (www.irmi.com).

Jack has personally written newsletters for his clients three times a year for more than 20 years. You can check out back issues of the newsletter, as well as subscribe to future electronic versions, at Jack's website (www.jackhungelmann.com). The site also contains Jack's contact information and links to most of his articles from the past several years.

Jack lives in Chaska, Minnesota, with his bride, Judy.